LIFE

A post-confirmation
course for teenagers

**DANNY CURTIN
& TOM CALUORI**

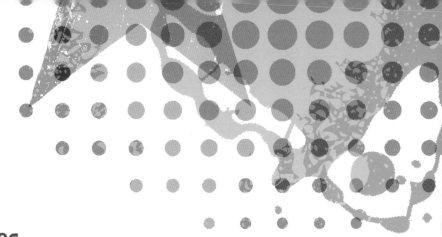

ABOUT THE AUTHORS

Tom Caluori has spent a lifetime working with young people, firstly as National Organiser for the Young Christian Workers movement in London and the southeast, then as a religious education specialist, Head of RE and School Chaplain. In 2003 Tom completed an MA in Pastoral Studies at Heythrop College, researching youth ministry. From 2003 to 2008 he worked as Youth Ministry Coordinator in Croydon Deanery and then as Chaplain at Croydon College of Further Education until 2012. Tom is now Chair of Croydon Deanery Youth Project and continues as Adult Companion to groups of teenagers.

Danny Curtin is the founder of the charity Million Minutes, a youth advocacy and fundraising charity, and has been very involved in Catholic youth work for over fifteen years. He served as National President of the Young Christian Workers (YCW) in England and Wales from 2005 to 2010 and now works with the international YCW team based in Rome, designing and supporting training of young leaders across the world. He also works with many charities in community work, disability, UK poverty, youth social exclusion, faith-based work and international development. Danny is also a magician, author and dedicated theatre fan.

ACKNOWLEDGEMENTS

The authors would like to thank Baroness Sheila Hollins for permission to use the Abuse/Grace model in Chapter 6.

Published by **Redemptorist Publications**
Alphonsus House, Chawton, Hampshire, GU34 3HQ, UK

A registered charity limited by guarantee
Registered in England 3261721
Copyright © Redemptorist Publications 2015
First published September 2015

Tel. +44 (0)1420 88222, Fax. +44 (0)1420 88805
Email rp@rpbooks.co.uk, www.rpbooks.co.uk

Text by Tom Caluori & Danny Curtin
Edited by Caroline Hodgson
Designed by Emma Hagan, Cover design by Louise Hilton
ISBN 978-0-85231-431-9

Printed by Portland Print, Kettering, NN16 8UN

CONTENTS

FOREWORD
ACCOMPANYING YOUNG PEOPLE

There is a well-known story told about a visitor to Ireland who pulls up at a crossroads and asks directions to Dublin from a local man. The man replies: "You could go straight ahead, take a left, then a right, then third right again, then straight over the roundabout, then left at the pub, then ask again... but if I were you I wouldn't start from here at all."

So often an adult considering the prospect of working with a group of young people, especially as they reach the teenage years, wonders where to start and reaches the conclusion: "I don't want to start from here – I want a nice number of well-mannered, appreciative, faith-filled, dedicated, responsible young people for my group".

Other adults may be tempted to take the well-worn phrase "Start where they are at!" as a recommendation to remain where they appear to be and never offer anything but bland acquiescence to their culture and values.

The fact is that young people are in two places at once. They are immersed in the reality of what it is to be a teenager in today's world with all its advantages and challenges, hopes and pressures, opportunities and disappointments. They are sons and daughters in families that can be close and supportive or dispersed and dysfunctional. They can so easily suffer from low self-image and lack of confidence that makes them shy and awkward. They are little protected from the power of the media, aggressive advertising and peer opinion. General secular social attitudes do not encourage them to be believers.

At the same time they are miracles of creative love, children of God, fashioned in God's own image with a sacred dignity and divine destiny. Within each is the capacity for amazing things.

An adult who sets out on the path of accompanying young people on their journey through these precious teenage years must hold both these two places in clear view and be convinced that accompaniment is a special art to be practised, worked upon, reflected on, improved upon and re-worked.

Pope Francis explicitly refers to this in his exhortation *Evangelii Gaudium* under the heading "Personal accompaniment in processes of growth":

In a culture paradoxically suffering from anonymity and at the same time obsessed with the details of other people's lives, shamelessly given over to morbid curiosity, the Church must look more closely and sympathetically at others whenever necessary. In our world, ordained ministers and other pastoral workers can make present the fragrance of Christ's closeness and his personal gaze. The Church will have to initiate everyone – priests, religious and laity – into this "art of accompaniment" which teaches us to remove our sandals before the sacred ground of the other.

Note the two phrases "to look more closely and sympathetically" and "to remove our sandals before the sacred ground of the other". See the truth of people's reality, accept the truth of faith.

Accompanying a group in this way is a formation for the lay apostolate, that is, the calling and mission of baptised lay people to transform the secular world. This may seem rather grandiose but it is a vocation that begins with relating faith to everyday circumstances and with very small steps of outgoing concern and friendship. The role of the adult companion towards the young people is illuminated by considering it under three aspects which follow on from one another but at the same time overlap considerably: to call, to form and to send out (Vocation, Formation and Mission). These are explored in the following introduction, but as we begin, take care not to approach this thinking that we are the ones who are going to do the calling forming and sending. Not at all. Remember that this is the Lord's work. We are there like John the Baptist to prepare the way, to grow smaller as he grows greater.

Mgr John Marsland
President of Ushaw College
National Chaplain to IMPACT/YCW

INTRODUCTION

Thank you for accompanying a group of young people on their journey of life and faith. Your dedication will speak volumes to them, not only about your commitment to young people, but also about the great worth the Church places on them, reflecting the unsurpassable love that God has for each and every one of them.

This practical expression of yours, showing young people that we care, and that they have a valued place in our communities, is the most important aspect of *Life*. You are beginning a journey with them which should be an exploration of life and faith. The Catholic Bishop's Conference of England and Wales, in their document on working with young people, says:

> *Catholic youth ministry accompanies young people through the transition from childhood to adulthood, so that they may deepen their encounter with Christ and be encouraged in faith, empowered with hope and supported in love to be the person they are called to be, now and in the future... The community provides nourishment for its young people so that they may encounter and come to know Christ.*
>
> **Called to a Noble Adventure, Catholic Bishop's Conference of England and Wales**

As the adult companion you are taking an active part in offering spiritual "nourishment" to the young people. Like so many of us you are probably very busy. You may or may not have prior experience of working with young people – and you wouldn't be alone if you were at a loss as to where to start.

The thought of starting a new initiative for a group of young people might well seem daunting, so an overall direction and methodology are essential. Based on many years of experience working with young people in the Church, this is the supportive framework that *Life* seeks to provide.

Life can be described as a formation programme for teenagers, but it can also be viewed as a tool to turn to (rather than a course to work through), to support you in accompanying the young people. The methodology within the themed chapters provides you with the foundational tools as you in turn walk alongside the young people and provide them with opportunities and encouragement as they reflect upon their lives in the light of faith. You will help them consider their hopes for the future, explore their influences and relationships, and discover their potential to contribute to the world.

THE ROLE OF THE ADULT COMPANION

A key task of the adult companion is to facilitate young people in their journey of self-discovery, to support and respect them as they go at their own pace. Like Eli awoken by Samuel, the adult companion enables the young people to listen to the word of God as it is addressed to them in the ordinary events of their lives.

If faith is to be real and if young people are to move to ownership of their faith, then it must resonate with them in their reality – their relationships, their culture and their everyday lives, so they can ask: "What is God calling me to in this moment?" Discernment in small groups, alongside one's peers, is an excellent starting point for this, and is at the heart of the method in *Life*.

There are three main elements to your role as adult companion. Although they are interwoven and happen at the same time, they also have a natural flow:

- *Calling* young people to consider their God-given purpose;

- *Forming* them in faith;

- *Sending* them out to transform the world.

TO CALL YOUNG PEOPLE (VOCATION)

The first call is the invitation to join the group – and the emphasis here should be on invitation. Of course we can still use the communication methods of the parish: a note in a newsletter or a notice at the back of church or in the school entrance hall. And, if your parish has the means, it could be a message on Twitter or a Facebook post (following safeguarding guidelines). But, if it is to be effective, there will most certainly be a personal element: a friend's face or voice, a prompt or invitation from someone they trust and respect.

This is the apparently random process through which the Lord will call some young people to start a significant journey. Be attentive and prayerful to notice those who might be open to God's call. They will not necessarily be the obvious ones. When you have identified some young people to invite, consider how to invite them and whether you are the best person to do it. Would the confirmation catechist, or the parishioner who helps with the football team be better placed to do it? The story of Jesus gathering his first disciples in John 1 gives interesting guidelines. His invitation is "Come and see." He does not embark on a thorough explanation of his mission – he encourages them to take a first step. They in turn bring others – Andrew brings Peter and Philip introduces Nathanael. We do not need to start with a crowd. Gather a few and let them "Come and see." The young people will bring others.

And they will come. They are waiting to be asked. They will come in response to a personal word of invitation, an expression of belief in what they have to offer or encouragement from their peer group. Call them for what you see within them. "We are starting a group, and I think you have something unique to bring to it," is so much stronger than an explanation burdened with tired church language. They can be helped by a chance to "give it a try" without making a full commitment, backed by wholehearted belief on our part that what is on offer is a great adventure.

The call is ongoing, it does not end when a young person joins a group. There is always another step, another challenge, to increase commitment, take on responsibility, reach out to others and grow in faith. Our task is to accompany this ongoing call.

TO FORM YOUNG PEOPLE (FORMATION)

Our wish is that young people will grow in faith, fulfil their potential and discover the riches of faith in Jesus Christ and of being a member of the Church. Do not impose your own faith on the young people, as each of them will be at a different point on his or her faith journey. A quiet, steady, no-frills affirmation of the fact that you are a believer in Christ without trying to impose any belief on or elicit any commitment from the young people, will give their faith room to flourish in its own time with God's grace and their openness.

The first requirement in accompanying a group is very simple: to be there. Your regular presence is already a big statement. It says, "I think you are worth it." Our presence needs to be consistent and also attentive. And we must be in it for the long haul. True growth takes time. We cannot expect quick results or immediate success.

Further to this underlying commitment and attentiveness there is need for a sound methodology of development. The insights and method of Joseph Cardijn, founder of the Young Christian Worker Movement, are presented in *Life* as a way of facing the real situations that young people experience and giving them a way forward inspired by the Gospel message and a closer relationship with Christ.

TO SEND YOUNG PEOPLE OUT (MISSION)

Being active, working together and achieving something concrete brings many benefits. It helps the group to gel, it increases confidence, gives a sense of responsibility and strengthens the group's identity. The role of the adult companion is to work behind the scenes and not to take on lots of the tasks. Often this involves the risk of things not being done or being done differently to how we would do it. Great patience and trust are required. At the same time you must be wise about what is realistic and give good advice when young people are planning an activity.

Two maxims were often repeated by Joseph Cardijn relating to action and responsibility:

- "Do it for them, do it with them and let them do it by themselves."

- "Always by the young people, never without the companion."

This is always the aim of the adult companion: that the young people take the reins – preparing the room, leading the meeting, saying the prayer, communicating to people outside the group, looking after the finances, making refreshments, clearing up after an event, reporting to the media. But it is always accompanied by our loving attention.

Life is recommended as a follow-up to parish confirmation catechesis when you have a ready-made group, some of whom may be keen to continue. Don't be tempted to take a break. Many parishes pause for the summer, thinking it is good to give the young people who have just been confirmed a rest. However, it usually proves very hard to re-gather the group at a later date. It is much more effective to work with the confirmation catechists to introduce *Life* immediately after confirmation, as an offer to those in the group who wish to continue meeting.

In addtion *Life* can be used with young people in a variety of other settings, e.g., within a school context, with those confirmed several years ago, or with teenagers who have not been confirmed.

THE PASTORAL CYCLE: A WAY OF LINKING EVERYDAY LIFE AND FAITH

Life uses the pastoral cycle approach to Christian formation: **SEE-JUDGE-ACT.** This is a tried-and-tested method of helping people to link their experience and faith through action. First developed by Cardinal Joseph Cardijn for the young people in the Young Christian Workers, since the Second Vatican Council it has been the method offered by the Church as the practical means to train lay people to live and act in the world.

> *Training for the apostolate cannot consist only in being taught theory; on that account there is need, right from the start of training, to learn gradually and prudently to see all things in the light of faith, to judge and act always in its light...*
>
> **Vatican II Decree on the Apostolate of Lay People**

It is a process of observing, discerning and planning action, forming young people to be aware of their surroundings, to reflect in faith, to ask what is good or bad about a situation and to move towards some kind of response in lived Christian action. The method gives young people responsibility and trains them in leadership.

> *Give me leaders and I will raise the world.*
>
> **Cardinal Joseph Cardijn**

Your role as the adult companion is to help the young people through the process of SEE, JUDGE and ACT. We do this through enquiry:

- First, we support young people to enquire into the events and circumstances of their lives and other people's.

- Next, we support them in enquiring into what the Christian view on these things might be.

- Finally we encourage them to enquire into what they can do about it.

The word "enquire" thereby sets the tone and encapsulates the methodology of the process. *Life* is structured as a series of "enquiries", which help the young people to **SEE**, **JUDGE** and **ACT**.

SEE

The **SEE** part of the enquiry takes as the starting point the young people themselves. The task of the adult companion is to encourage them to share their own situations and those of people they know. They may share a situation, conversation or event from their daily life. What they share should be real and factual. It should have made them think a little, feel good or bad, get angry or want to help someone. The questions asked will begin *What?, Who?, How?*

JUDGE

Then follows a discernment or reflection upon the situations and events that have been **SEEN**, in the **JUDGE** stage of the enquiry. Key questions will include: What do we think about this? Is this good or bad? Is this right or wrong? Why/why not? What is the Christian view?

The **JUDGE** includes an enquiry into a Gospel passage, which can be applied to the situation shared within the group. The main thrust of this part of the enquiry is: "Could/should things be different? If so, how?"

ACT

SEEING and **JUDGING** should always lead to **ACTION**. Action can be taken by individual members or the group as whole. The **ACT** part of the enquiry is crucial if the group is not to be merely a talking shop. It is through the actions decided upon and carried out that the young people grow and begin to see Christianity as relevant to daily living. After all, the aim of the adult companion is to walk with the young people as they grow in faith to become fully mature Christians with a sense of mission.

Action can be seen in terms of **serving**, **educating** and **representing**. Service means carrying out some kind of action to meet a need. Education is about raising the awareness of others. Representation is about standing up for those in need and bringing the matters that have arisen to the attention of those with the ability to bring about change. It is about being a prophetic voice.

In the *Life* enquiries, **serve**, **educate** and **represent** are referred to as **HELP**, **TELL IT** and **STAND UP**.

REVIEW

After the first enquiry, each subsequent enquiry includes a **review** of what has gone before. Whether things go right or wrong it is always good to review what has happened. Where there is success, it needs to be celebrated, recognised and affirmed, to give the young people confidence and a sense of real achievement. Where things do not work out, it is good to help them pick up the pieces, learn from mistakes and see the good that did happen. Remember that every step is a big victory.

The adult companion should look for opportunities for the young people to review their actions, their responsibilities and the deeper meaning of what they are involved in.

RECORD SHEETS

The **record sheet** is crucial for the review, and for the success of any agreed action. Taking notes signifies the seriousness of the meeting and enables the group to check on progress. Every time something is agreed, a member of the group should take notes of any issues raised, any conclusions reached and any actions that have been decided.

If you are working with several smaller groups, each should have a note-taker who can use the record sheets and then report back to the whole group. Ideally this task will be allocated to a different person at each meeting or enquiry — you may want to encourage the young people to discuss and decide the best approach for themselves.

In addition, you will find it important to keep your own record of anything that has been said and agreed. It could be that you keep the flipchart paper — you may well find that notes get lost between meetings and it will be very useful to have your own as a backup!

CIRCLE OF INFLUENCE

A central theme to this programme is encouraging the young people to identify where they can be a positive influence in people's lives and thereby grow as young Christian leaders.

The **Circle of Influence** chart is completed in the second enquiry and offers a tool to help the young people reflect on their lives and opportunities for action. When they are considering how each theme impacts upon their own experience at the **SEE** stage, the chart can help to expand their thinking to consider the friends, family, peers and even strangers who play a part in their lives. Similarly, at the **ACT** stage, a glance at the **Circle of Influence** chart will remind them of those people and help them think about who is in need of support. Encourage group members to update their chart regularly to include new people who have come into their circle of influence.

When the young people are considering how to respond to the people on their chart, small things are very important: a kindly gesture, a supportive comment, a useful question, a bit of time sacrificed, a responsibility fulfilled. The adult companion can help to affirm these kinds of actions in relation to the young people's family, friends and contacts.

YOUNG PEOPLE LEAD

It is the adult companion's role always to seek to give young people responsibility, no matter how small, so as to encourage their sense of self-worth. For example, when the group first meets, the adult companion will need to ask the questions during the enquiries to enable the young people to share sensibly and ensure that the process is followed. However, as soon as is practical, and ideally in the second meeting, the adult companion should offer this responsibility to the young people, encouraging members to take turns in leading the enquiry. You should meet the young people who will lead in advance of each meeting. This can be done at the end of the meeting before, or during free time between meetings.

The young person who is leading will ask the questions during the enquiry (**SEE**, **JUDGE** and

ACT). Be clear that it will be their role, with your support, to encourage and enable all the members of the group to contribute. This is a difficult task for some young people and should be approached with care. In your preparation encourage the young leader to imagine how the session will unfold. How will people in the group react to the questions? Which questions might be difficult? Who might need encouragement? What follow-up questions might be useful?

The young people may need encouragement to share. At this point the leader may find it helpful to ask very direct questions, e.g., "Do we have friends who have experienced that?" Help the young leader to think of likely situations the young people may respond to, to get them started. Another tip is to suggest discussing a topic in pairs before they share with the whole group.

In addition to the young person leading the enquiry, there are other opportunities to get members of the group involved. They can be invited to read the Gospel passage and also the stories that recount young people's experiences. Be sure to allow any readers time to prepare their reading if they wish.

PRAYER TIME

The time at the end of each enquiry is devoted to bringing the insights, reflections and commitments together in prayer. A format is offered for you in each chapter.

This should last around seven minutes. Too long and you will lose the young people's attention, yet it should allow enough time to enable what has happened in the meeting to "settle" into the group.

The best approach is to connect the prayer with the theme of the session rather than making it a "bolt-on" exercise. However, there may be occasions – such as when a session has been particularly intense or challenging – when you can see that it needs a different approach.

The aim here is to introduce prayer as an organic part of daily life rather than a pious, perfunctory exercise.

Following are some suggestions for prayer time:

- Background music may help to provide a prayerful setting. Note, however, that you may need to check with the venue that the appropriate licences are in place.

- Sample stories and applications are included in this book. However, if you can think of one that is more appropriate for the group, use that instead. Ideally it would be read by one of the young people.

- The prayer time concludes with a closing prayer from the young people's booklet and a blessing said together or given by a member of the clergy if present. There are books with blessings available but the following is a good example: "May the grace of our Lord Jesus Christ the Love of God the fellowship of the Holy Spirit be with us all, now and evermore" (2 Corinthians 13:13).

- The closing prayer includes an invitation for the Holy Spirit to come. Young people who have been confirmed have received the Holy Spirit sacramentally, but all can pray for the Holy Spirit to come, asking for whatever gifts are needed. The young people can be empowered to live as fully alive members of the Church. The purpose of *Life* is to help the young people to see what this might mean in practice. They should be reminded to call upon the Holy Spirit to empower them each day as they grow as young Christian leaders.

PRACTICALITIES

SAFEGUARDING

Before you begin inviting young people into a group, speak to the safeguarding representative in your parish to ensure that you are aware of all the procedures you need to follow to work with young people below the age of eighteen. As well as being safely recruited to your role as adult companion (which will involve a check of your criminal record) you will need to be familiar with the good practice guidelines of how to work with young people and to create and maintain a safe and supportive environment.

One of these guidelines is the required adult-to-young person ratio. For a small group of teenagers this usually means two adults working alongside one another. The other adult may not need to take on the same responsibility as you (although it is good if they do). They could, for example, welcome the young people and prepare the room, without taking on an accompanying role. However, they should be present so that you are never in a situation where you will be left alone with just one young person.

THE GROUP

Generally six to ten young people is a good number for group sharing. If there are more young people coming to the meeting, smaller groups may need to be formed as part of the session, with young people in each small group taking responsibility to lead the enquiries.

TIMING

It is highly recommended that the group meets every week at a set time and place to ensure continuity. Enquiries may be approached in two main ways; either taking one enquiry each week or else over three weeks – **SEE** the first week, then **JUDGE** the second, and finally **ACT** on the third week.

To cover all aspects of the enquiry in one meeting would take approximately one and a half hours depending upon the group. To take the enquiry over three weeks would allow more time for each stage, as well as some social time.

Social time is an opportunity for the young people to develop friendships within the group, to relax and build a sense of belonging. Music and refreshments should be provided by the young people. Someone can be chosen to collect a small subscription each week to pay for this. The weekly sub also helps the group to feel that it is their group.

THE PLACE AND MATERIALS

At the beginning of the first session, the meeting area should be set up ready for prayer with chairs in a circle and somewhere to place the basket for the individual prayers. If you are working with a single group you might want to use a flipchart and marker pens. In subsequent sessions you can invite the young people to prepare the space. Slips of paper and pencils should be at hand. A candle or other suitable focus (such as an open Bible) is placed in the centre as a reminder of God's presence.

TIPS FOR ADULT COMPANIONS

- Pray for the young people and for the gifts to be an effective adult companion. The following prayer, similar to the suggested concluding prayer in each chapter, may be helpful to your own prayerful preparation:

PRAYER FOR YOUNG PEOPLE

Father, pour out your Spirit

upon our young people,

and grant them

a new vision of your glory,

a new experience of your power,

a new faithfulness to your Word; and

a new consecration to your service,

that your love may grow in them,

and your kingdom come.

Through Christ our Lord.

Amen.

- Prepare the meeting by going carefully through the enquiry beforehand; try to anticipate any problems or sensitivities that may arise.

- Begin the meeting with a prayer and invite the young people to offer their own intentions – some guidance may be needed here.

- There are ice-breakers suggested to begin each new chapter, and extras in the Appendix if enquiries stretch over several meetings. This informal start, with an ice-breaker or game, is always a good idea. It helps the young people to lighten up and get to know one another better.

- Ask for a report from the young people of any action arising from the previous meeting. Ensure that the action is noted.

- Before beginning each enquiry, the questions asked in the the **News Round** section invite the young people to review their recent experiences and raise any concerns which are not necessarily relevant to the session topic. Keep this brief but with due respect to the young people who are brave enough to share. If the group wishes to follow up anything which is shared, use the guide in the Appendix to accompany them in this process.

- For the enquiry proper, if necessary divide the group into smaller groups of about six to ten. Do this by giving each person a number so that it is not just friendship groups and that no

one feels left out. Keep the groups the same as far as possible each week. This is important so that issues can be properly followed up.

- Encourage each group to appoint a note-taker and someone to lead the enquiry. Arrange to meet the young person who will be leading this meeting beforehand to prepare.

- The young people should be asked to speak one at a time and to listen respectfully to each other. The quiet ones especially will not speak up if they fear being ridiculed or made fun of.

- The young people must be free not to contribute, but gently encouraged to do so. Encourage the group to respect confidentiality.

- The adult companion should offer confidentiality to the group and also insist on it from the group. However, if you consider that a young person's safety is at risk, you may need to seek guidance from a professional body, such as the police or Health Service.

- The more vocal group members may need to be encouraged to give others the opportunity to speak. A good tip is to ask the more vocal members to lead the enquiry. Use your preparation time with them to emphasise the importance of encouraging each member to speak if they wish.

Giving them the responsibility to manage other people's participation will often discourage the leader from speaking too much.

- As well as encouraging the young people to make notes for reflection and follow-up at each meeting, take notes of your own, to enable you to check and confirm what has been said and agreed.

VISION FOR YOUTH MINISTRY

We cherish young people for who they are now, for all the energy, gifts, joys and challenges that they bring to our communities and for who they are to become. Young people are both our present and our future. During this period of their lives they have a unique role to play and a unique voice to be heard. Young people should enjoy happy and healthy lives, with the support, love and encouragement needed for each one of them to grow into faithful adults in love with Christ and committed to the building of the kingdom of God.

Called to a Noble Adventure, Catholic Bishop's Conference of England and Wales.

HOPES AND DREAMS

ADULT COMPANION'S REFLECTION

In this first session the young people begin to get to know one another (or continue to develop friendships they formed in their Confirmation group or school). Encourage the young people to have fun as well as to be challenged. The session is about them, their hopes and dreams, gifts and talents. Can you recall your own hopes and dreams when you were their age? What were the things that worried you? No doubt you can look back now and realise you have learnt so much since then, and have so much advice to offer others. However, resist the temptation to judge the hopes and dreams of the young people, or to "correct" what they say and think.

As their adult companion you'll start this journey in a privileged position, walking with them as they journey through the coming weeks discovering together how their faith can help them achieve their potential and make a real difference in the world. This first chapter is the foundation for that journey.

TIP

If you are accompanying the group as a team of adults, try to meet for a few minutes before each session and read and think through the leader's introduction.

Invite the group to be quiet. Offer each person an opportunity to name an intention (such as a name or situation). Bring all these together in saying a prayer together:

PRAYER

Father, pour out your Holy Spirit upon us

your sons and daughters.

May we see with your eyes,

judge all things in your light

and act with love in our hearts.

Mould us into your apostles

full of joy and hope,

so that we can be the difference

and your kingdom come

and keep us under your protection.

Through Christ Jesus our friend and Saviour.

Amen.

There is an alternative prayer suggested in the last chapter of the young people's book:

PRAYER

Lord Jesus,

We thank you for this day.

We offer you all our hopes and struggles, joys and sorrows.

Help us to grow together in friendship,

so that our words and actions bear witness to you

and make a difference in people's lives.

We pray for our families, for those who are hungry, lonely, poor and homeless,

and for all who have asked for our prayers.

May you bless us with wisdom to care for the earth.

May you bless us in love to care for one another.

In your name may we make all things new.

Amen.

If the young people do not know one another – begin by inviting each individual to introduce themselves:

- What school do you go to?

- What year group are you in?

ICE-BREAKER – LIKES AND DISLIKES NAME GAME

Use the following ice-breaker, or another of your choice (a selection of alternatives can be found in the Appendices).

Ask each person to say their name and an adjective which signifies how they see themselves or the person they would like to be (it can be a fun or self-mocking title), e.g. Terrible Tom, Likeable Lucy. Start with a suggestion of your own.

A like or dislike is then added, e.g. "Terrible Tom and I support Chelsea FC"; "Likeable Lucy and I hate cabbage".

When it comes to each person's turn, they introduce themselves and then repeat what all the previous people have said. The last person to contribute has the hardest task of course!

You can also use a tennis ball to select who will speak next. After the first person has spoken they select the next speaker by throwing the ball to them. This makes is even harder, as each person has to remember the order in which people have spoken, as well as remembering their name and like/dislike.

GETTING STARTED

When you have finished go around the group one more time and give everyone the chance to answer the following questions:

- Why have we come here today?
- What are our hopes for this group?

ENQUIRY

NOTE: If you complete an enquiry over several meetings, the Prayer, News Round and Review should be repeated at the beginning of each session.

ENQUIRY SUMMARY – SEE, JUDGE, ACT

Each enquiry has a central narrative, or flow, which can be summarised with a few questions. In each chapter we'll provide you with this summary to help you prepare and focus for your meetings:

SEE – What are our hopes, dreams and gifts?

JUDGE – How important is it that we have good dreams, and use our gifts well?

ACT – How can we use of gifts for one another?

Each week we look at (**SEE**) what is happening in our lives, **JUDGE** whether situations are good or bad in light of faith, and then decide how to **ACT** – what we can do to improve things, in other words, to be the difference.

SEE

Explain to the group that each meeting will start with **SEE** – looking at something real and factual. This will include looking at events in the young people's real lives, what makes them happy, and the difficulties and problems they face.

Stress that it is important from the start to respect one another, listening to what others have to say. There needs to be an atmosphere of trust in the group, so that people feel free to speak about what is happening to them and say what is on their minds.

Explain that this week you, as the adult companion, will ask the questions, but in future weeks a group member should ask the questions. (As the adult companion you should prepare each session in advance with the young person who is leading.)

As you begin the session, encourage everyone to take notes in their book. Ask someone to take notes on the record sheet or flipchart paper so that everyone can see it.

- What are our hopes and dreams for the future?
- What gets in the way of us achieving our dreams?

TIP

If people find it difficult to share with the whole group straight away, invite the group to first make a few notes for themselves in their book. They can then share what they have written with one other person, before sharing with the whole group. This helps everyone to engage and encourages individuals within the group to share.

GIFTS

- What are the good things that your friends or family would say about you?
- What gifts can you identify in yourself? Look at the list below to help you.

NOTES

Loving	Imaginative
Leadership	Caring
Humour	Popular
Courage	Confident
Beauty	A good friend
Fun	Intelligent
Inspiring	Close family ties
Inquisitive	Loyal to others
Decisive	Generous
Helpful	Brave
Creative	Athletic
A good listener	Musical
Reliable	Artistic
Wise	Honest

Invite each member to comment about the gifts they have chosen. Can other members of the group help to identify additional gifts in them? Then ask the group:

- How can these gifts help you to achieve your dreams?

Whatever you are, be a good one.

Abraham Lincoln

JUDGE

Explain to the group that once they have seen what's really happening it is time to move on to **JUDGE**. This is the time when the young people explore what they think about these issues, what's good or bad about the situations, and what their faith says.

- Do our hopes and dreams for ourselves also contribute to the good of others?

- Does it matter if some of our dreams are "selfish"? If so, why? If not, why not?

GOSPEL ENQUIRY

Invite a young person (who should have had a chance to prepare) to read the Gospel passage aloud. Ask the group to listen carefully to the story and think about the time, place and people involved.

Time allowing, it can be a good idea to invite a second young person to re-read the passage, although again ensure that she or he has had a chance to prepare it.

MATTHEW 25:14-30

For it is as if a man, going on a journey, summoned his slaves and entrusted his property to them; to one he gave five talents, to another two, to another one, to each according to his ability. Then he went away. The one who had received the five talents went off at once and traded with them, and made five more talents. In the same way, the one who had the two talents made two more talents. But the one who had received the one talent went off and dug a hole in the ground and hid his master's money. After a long time the master of those slaves came and settled accounts with them. Then the one who had received the five talents came forward, bringing five more talents, saying, "Master, you handed over to me five talents; see, I have made five more talents." His master said to him, "Well done, good and trustworthy slave; you have been trustworthy in a few things, I will put you in charge of many things; enter into the joy of your master." And the one with the two talents also came forward, saying, "Master, you handed over to me two talents; see, I have made two more talents." His master said to him, "Well done, good and trustworthy slave; you have been trustworthy in a few things, I will put you in charge of many things; enter into the joy of your master." Then the one who had received the one talent also came forward, saying, "Master, I knew that you were a harsh man, reaping where you did not sow, and gathering where you did not scatter seed; so I was afraid, and I went and hid your talent in the ground. Here you have what is yours." But his master replied, "You wicked and lazy slave! You knew, did you, that I reap where I did not sow, and gather where I did not scatter? Then you ought to have invested my money with the bankers, and on my return I would have received what was my own with interest. So take the talent from him, and give it to the one with the ten talents. For to all those who have, more will be given, and they will have an abundance; but from those who have nothing, even what they have will be taken away. As for this worthless slave, throw him into the outer darkness, where there will be weeping and gnashing of teeth."

- Who is in this story and what happened?

- What was said? How do you think the people present would have reacted? Why?

In the time of Jesus a talent was worth more than fifteen years' wages of a worker. It's a precious thing – a gift given for a purpose. This parable shows us that the "master" wants us to do well with our gifts, and that we should use all our gifts for good, not just for ourselves but for others.

- Jesus' parable invites us to consider how we use our gifts for others, rather than keeping them to ourselves. Do you use your gifts unselfishly and to the full? How can you use them for others?

- Look back at the gifts you identified in **SEE**. Which gifts has God given you? How could you use them better to achieve God's hopes and dreams for you?

- Can you think of other gifts which God has given you? If you have been confirmed, do you remember the gifts of the Holy Spirit?

- Are God's hopes and dreams for us the same as our hopes and dreams for ourselves?

BEING CONFIRMED

Look at the gifts of the Spirit below which are received at the sacrament of Confirmation:

GIFTS OF THE HOLY SPIRIT

WISDOM and UNDERSTANDING

To help us see things through the eyes of Jesus and to understand how to love God and others.

RIGHT JUDGEMENT and COURAGE

To make the right choices and to have courage to live the values of the Gospel each day.

KNOWLEDGE and REVERENCE

To know God and have a sense of beauty and respect for all God has created.

WONDER and AWE

To see God in the world and to value God's plan for us.

- Are these gifts important in your life? Why?

- How might these gifts help you to achieve your hopes and dreams?

ACT

Explain to the group that our seeing and judging always leads us to action.

By committing to take action after we finish our enquiry we are saying that we want to make a difference in our lives and the lives of others. We are committing to living as disciples of Jesus.

- What action can we take following our enquiry?

- How will we use our gifts and talents for good this week?

Now you are the body of Christ and individually members of it.

1 Corinthians 12:27

In each chapter we will consider action in three categories:

HELP – Helping others through service.

TELL IT – Making others aware of what we have discovered.

STAND UP – Standing up on behalf of others who do not or cannot speak out for themselves.

This week we focus on HELP – and how you can play your full role in your parish community.

NOTES

HELP

Encourage each young person to consider how they can become involved members of the parish.

Is anyone already involved in the parish in any way? For example as a server, reader, in a sports team or helping at the youth club?

Think about your gifts and talents. Which of the following would suit you?

- Taking part in Mass as a server or reader.

- Helping with children's liturgy, first Communion preparation, the coffee morning, a fundraising event, or a piety/book stall.

- Offering service to those in need — for example in a Justice and Peace group, a Traidcraft stall, visiting older members of the parish, or helping at an older people's club.

- Becoming involved in the parish music ministry.

- Volunteering for the church's welcome ministry.

- Supporting people with learning disabilities, either through a church group or another organisation (the adult companion should be able to advise which one would be suitable).

- Supporting younger people — such as by helping in a children's group or youth club.

- Taking part in charitable sporting activities.

- Becoming involved with your parish council.

Make a note to contact the relevant person before next week, to ask if you can help.

TELL IT

This is about raising awareness, or drawing people's attention to something they should be aware of.

- Do we want to keep meeting as a group? Could you tell other young people about this group and invite them along. If so, make a note of who to contact.

STAND UP

This is about standing up on behalf of others who do not speak out for themselves. You might decide to:

- Speak to the parish priest or to the parish council about the importance of your group and of inviting young people to be involved in the parish.

What action or actions have you committed to? Write them down and ask the adult companion if you need help making contact with anyone.

Invite the young people to commit to taking an action and to sharing their commitment with the group.

The actions should be noted on the flipchart or record sheet. You will need to keep these notes safe to enable the group to look back next time to check what action has been carried out and to give continuity to the meetings.

REACH OUT AND LIVE LIFE!

Help the group to identify where they can make a difference.

At the end of the programme, Chapter Eight will invite you to design a group project to **REACH OUT AND LIVE LIFE!** Over the coming weeks, as a group you should decide what issue or issues you want to act upon. Where can you make a difference as a group? Make a note to return to in Chapter Eight:

- Has this enquiry given you any ideas for your group project?

- Make a note in your book — ideas for group project.

- As individuals, commit to think and pray about your group project between now and the next session.

Invite the young people to give thought and prayer to the group project in the time between now and the next session.

PRAYER TIME

Light a candle in the middle of the room, with the young people sitting around in a circle. Remind the group that this is a sign of God's presence. Play some quiet music in the background.

USING OUR GIFTS TO BUILD OUR FUTURE

Read by someone in the group.

There was once a builder who was very good at his trade but eventually the time came for him to retire from work. He went to his boss and told him this. The boss was naturally very upset to be losing such a fine craftsman. Nevertheless the boss said to the builder, "Look there is one last job I would like you to do. One last house I would like you to build."

The builder agreed and set about his work. However his heart wasn't in it and very soon he was cutting corners, using inferior materials and doing shoddy work.

When the builder had finished, the boss came to see the work and he handed the keys to the builder saying that the house was his gift to him for his retirement. The builder was of course gutted. If he had only known he would have made the house his best effort ever but it was too late and there was no going back.

Author unknown

APPLICATION

God is the master builder and we are called to use our gifts and talents which God has given us to build our future. This is a work for each day and each week. If we put our trust in God to lead us we will achieve our full potential in God's plan. In so doing we will be the difference to all those around us and in society at large. This is what these meetings are all about.

PRAYER

Pass around slips of paper and pens. Invite each of the young people to compose a prayer to place in a basket, which is then placed in the centre.

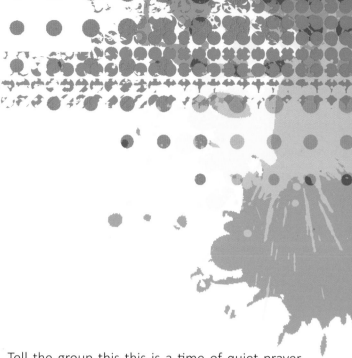

Tell the group this this is a time of quiet prayer and reflection, in which they may ask for God's direction in how to support someone in need, or how to ask someone for help if they are in need themselves.

Invite the group to say the following prayer together from their books:

CLOSING PRAYER

Father, pour out your Spirit

upon your young people,

and grant us

a new vision of your glory,

a new experience of your power,

a new faithfulness to your Word; and

a new consecration to your service,

that your love may grow in us,

and your kingdom come.

Through Christ our Lord.

Amen.

SOCIAL TIME

10-20 minutes.

As the adult companion you may want to provide some refreshments this week but the young people can take turns in the future. Alternatively, all the young people may contribute a small amount of money (it is good to give the young people some responsibility and encourage ownership of their group). Bring some speakers to allow the young people to plug in their music.

RECORD SHEET

2

CIRCLES OF INFLUENCE

ADULT COMPANION'S REFLECTION

Life keeps getting faster and busier and it is all too easy to bypass the important while we are so caught up with the urgent. How often do you find yourself thinking that you must find time to catch up with an old friend, or phone a relative? How rarely do you find time to reach beyond your ready-made circle of friends and acquaintances, to get to know someone a bit better? It could be the girl who works in a shop you regularly buy milk in, or an old man you often see at the bus stop.

Despite living in a "connected" world, with modern technology at our fingertips which seemingly keeps us in touch with one another, we often forget the importance of being present to those around us, and responding to the needs of those in our Circle of Influence.

This session invites the young people to consider their Circles of Influence – both in terms of people whose lives they touch, and in terms of those who touch their lives. Who do they feel close to? Who can they talk to? Who do they see each day but might take for granted? Is there anyone they are connected with emotionally, but far away from geographically?

The Circle of Influence chart is a powerful practical tool to enable the young people to consider who might be in need of support, and to look at the network of support available to them when they are in need. Whether it is responding to the loneliness of a new classmate, or offering friendship to an elderly neighbour, this chapter will help us take stock and identify who is in our lives, and how we can live the call of the Gospel among them.

If young people are not already leading the sessions, invite one or two to lead. (For more on this refer to the Introduction. You will for example need to sit down with them before the session to help them prepare. Look at the questions for discussion and help the young people imagine how the session may develop.)

Invite the group to be quiet. Offer each person an opportunity to name an intention (such as a name or situation). Bring all these intentions together in saying a prayer:

PRAYER

Father, pour out your Holy Spirit upon us

your sons and daughters.

May we see with your eyes,

judge all things in your light

and act with love in our hearts.

Mould us into your apostles

full of joy and hope,

so that we can be the difference

and your kingdom come

and keep us under your protection.

Through Christ Jesus our friend and Saviour.

Amen.

There is also an alternative prayer suggested in the last chapter of the young people's book:

PRAYER

Lord Jesus,

We thank you for this day.

We offer you all our hopes and struggles, joys and sorrows.

Help us to grow together in friendship,

so that our words and actions bear witness to you

and make a difference in people's lives.

We pray for our families, for those who are hungry, lonely, poor and homeless,

and for all you have asked for our prayers.

May you bless us with wisdom to care for the earth.

May you bless us in love to care for one another.

In your name may we make all things new.

Amen.

ICE-BREAKER – TWO TRUTHS AND A LIE

Use the following ice-breaker, or another of your choice (a selection of alternatives can be found in the Appendices).

Invite each person in turn to say three things about themselves – two of which are true and one is untrue. The other members of the group in turn will then say which of the three statements is a lie. When everyone has given their verdict the person should own up to their lie. Start with a suggestion of your own.

The aim is to fool everyone in the group. The one who fools the most in the group is the winner. Apart from great fun the game helps the group to get to know one another a little better.

The trick is to make the lie believable and choose the most incredible true things about oneself, for example:

- I am in the school football team.

- I went on holiday to Spain last year.

- I came last in my end-of-year maths test last year.

Any one of these could be true. The more out of the ordinary the examples are, the more fun it is.

NEWS ROUND

- What has happened to you this week?

- Share one fact from your week (a good or bad thing). What has made you think, caused you concern or given you reason to celebrate?

NOTE: If something significant comes up, it may be more important to follow it up than to complete today's enquiry. If you need to follow up on anything you can use the short enquiry approach found in the Appendices.

REVIEW

Invite the group to look at last week's record sheet or flipchart sheets. Ask the young people to share the results of their actions.

Look back at the last time you met. Hold one another to account:

- What individual or group actions did you decide upon?

- Were these actions carried out?

- If so, how did it go?

- Did you choose a role in the parish to participate in?

- If so, what have you done to begin?

ENQUIRY

NOTE: If you complete an enquiry over several meetings, the Prayer, News Round and Review should be repeated at the beginning of each session.

Each enquiry has a central narrative, or flow, which can be summarised with a few questions. In each chapter we'll provide you with this summary to help you prepare and focus for your meetings:

SEE – Who is in our Circle of Influence?

JUDGE – Do we have resposibility for others?

ACT – How can we **HELP**, **TELL IT** or **STAND UP** for people in our Circle of Influence?

SEE

As you begin the session, encourage everyone to take notes in their book. Ask someone to take notes on the record sheet or flipchart paper so that everyone can see it.

- Who do you live with? Who would you regard as your family?

- How many of your friends would you call close or best friends?

- Apart from close friends, who else do you have regular contact with?

YOUR CIRCLE OF INFLUENCE

Invite the young people to work in pairs to each complete a Circle of Influence chart.

Working in pairs, each complete a Circle of Influence chart. Complete each section in turn:

- Who are you in regular contact with in your home and family?

- Who are your friends? Who do you see in your leisure time?

- Who do you spend time with at school, in college, or doing a part-time job?

- Who do you spend time with in your neighbourhood? Do you go to any groups, clubs, or other local activities?

- Who do you see regularly but don't know? That could be, for example, someone who works in a shop you regularly go into, a bus driver or receptionist in the doctor's surgery.

- How do you think of them as different to, for example, people you would count as friends and family? Do you think this person thinks of you in a similar way?

FRIENDS & CONTACTS

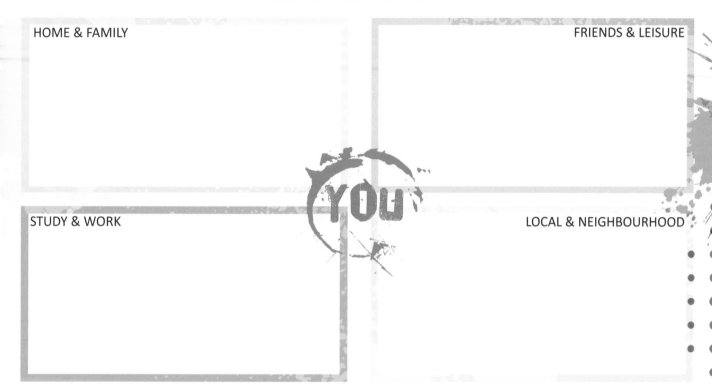

HOME & FAMILY

FRIENDS & LEISURE

STUDY & WORK

LOCAL & NEIGHBOURHOOD

Read and discuss the following examples of situations (if time is limited you may want to pick two or three):

- Steve's parents have moved the family to a new town and he is starting a new school.

- Rosemary thinks that she doesn't belong because of the way she speaks.

- Toby is trying to stop drinking as much, but his friends tell him he's just boring.

- Jo is starting a new part-time job, so she at least has some money to go out with friends.

- Kathryn's accident led to a disability. Her friends drifted away and now she's being bullied.

- Rick keeps getting upset, and doesn't know how to hide it at school, because his parents are rowing and talking about divorce.

- Rach loves her boyfriend, but she thinks her family will disapprove, so she still hasn't told them about him.

In each case consider:

- How do you think Steve, Rosemary, Toby, Jo, Kathryn, Rick or Rach feel in these situations?

- How do you think people in their Circle of Influence feel about the situation?

Look at the names on your Circle of Influence chart and consider the following:

- Do you know anyone facing a difficult or stressful situation? It could be to do with bullying, peer pressure, problems at home.

- Could you do or have done anything more, or anything differently, to help?

- When have you needed help and support from those in your Circle of Influence? Did it help and if so how?

- Have you experienced someone trying to help when in fact it had the opposite effect?

NOTE: Be clear that nobody needs to talk about anything they're not comfortable with, and not to disclose any names or identifying details.

NOTES

Lord your God with all your heart, and with all your soul, and with all your strength, and with all your mind; and your neighbour as yourself." And he said to him, "You have given the right answer; do this, and you will live." But wanting to justify himself, he asked Jesus, "And who is my neighbour?" Jesus replied, "A man was going down from Jerusalem to Jericho, and fell into the hands of robbers, who stripped him, beat him, and went away, leaving him half dead. Now by chance a priest was going down that road; and when he saw him, he passed by on the other side. So likewise a Levite, when he came to the place and saw him, passed by on the other side. But a Samaritan while traveling came near him; and when he saw him, he was moved with pity. He went to him and bandaged his wounds, having poured oil and wine on them. Then he put him on his own animal, brought him to an inn, and took care of him. The next day he took out two denarii, gave them to the innkeeper, and said, "Take care of him; and when I come back, I will repay you whatever more you spend.' Which of these three, do you think, was a neighbour to the man who fell into the hands of the robbers?" He said, "The one who showed him mercy." Jesus said to him, "Go and do likewise."

JUDGE

NOTE: In encouraging the young people to judge these situations, encourage them to think about those at the centre of their Circle of Influence (close friends, family, etc.) as well as others on the periphery.

- What do you think about the situations you have discussed? Is there anything wrong or unjust about them?

- What should a healthy Circle of Influence look like?

- How are we called to support other people in our Circle of Influence?

- How do we want other people in our Circle of Influence to treat us? Can we understand why they sometimes don't?

GOSPEL ENQUIRY

Invite a young person (who should have had a chance to prepare) to read the Gospel passage aloud. Ask the group to listen carefully to the story and think about the time, place and people involved.

Time allowing, it can be a good idea to invite a second young person to re-read the passage, although again ensure that she or he has also had a chance to prepare it.

LUKE 10:25-37

Just then a lawyer stood up to test Jesus. "Teacher," he said, "what must I do to inherit eternal life?" He said to him, "What is written in the law? What do you read there?" He answered, "You shall love the

- What happened in the story? Who passed by the man in his time of need?

- Why do you think they might have done this?

- Can you relate this story to the situations you have been looking at, or to your own experience? Has anyone ever "passed by" you in a time of need? Have you done the same to someone who might have needed help?

ACT

In everything I did, I showed you that by this kind of hard work we must help the weak, remembering the words the Lord Jesus himself said: "It is more blessed to give than to receive".

Acts 20:35

By committing to take action after we finish our enquiry we are saying that we want to make a difference in our lives and the lives of others. We are committing to living as disciples of Jesus.

In each chapter we will consider action in three categories:

HELP – *Helping others through service.*

TELL IT – *Making others aware of what we have discovered.*

STAND UP – *Standing up on behalf of others who do not or cannot speak out for themselves.*

As a group, think about a specific situation – probably from something you have been discussing today – which causes you concern. Could you – either as a group or as individuals – do anything to **HELP, TELL IT** or **STAND UP**?

HELP

This is about helping and supporting other people, and deepening our relationships. You could for example:

- Look at your Circle of Influence and give thought and prayer to whether there is any way in which you could help a friend in a difficult situation.

- Consider those less known to you. There may be someone on the edge of your Circle of Influence who you don't know very well, but who might benefit from your support. How could you offer your help to them? Could you get to know them better?

TELL IT

This is about raising awareness, or drawing people's attention to something they should know about. You could for example:

- Find out more about the situations you have looked at which affect young people in terms of relationships.

- Collect and distribute information about the problems which affect young people.

- Organise a talk for your group, club or school.

- Talk to someone who seems lonely and consider whether it would be appropriate to get to know them better, or to invite them to join in an activity

you take part in. Bear in mind that the answer may sometimes be that it is not appropriate!

STAND UP

This is about standing up for ourselves, or on behalf of others who do not or cannot speak out for themselves. The young people might decide to:

- Stand up for someone who is being bullied. Bear in mind that drawing attention to it could be counter-productive. So pray about the alternatives. You could offer them support by simply letting them know that you care, by talking to them, or helping them to get other appropriate support. These are all ways of standing up for someone.

Invite the young people to commit to taking an action and to sharing their commitment with the group.

What action or actions have you committed to? How are you going to make a start?

The actions should be noted on the flipchart or record sheet. You will need to keep these notes safe to enable the group to look back next time to check what action has been carried out and to give continuity to the meetings.

REACH OUT AND LIVE LIFE!

Help the group to identify where they can make a difference.

At the end of the programme, Chapter Eight will invite the group to design a project to **REACH OUT AND LIVE LIFE!** Over the coming weeks, the group should decide what issue or issues to act upon.

Where can you make a difference as a group? Make a note to return to in Chapter Eight:

- Has this enquiry given you any ideas for your group project?

- Make a note in your book – ideas for group project.

- As individuals, commit to think and pray about your group project between now and the next session.

Invite the young people to give thought and prayer time to the group project in the time between now and the next session.

PRAYER TIME

Light a candle in the middle of the room, with the young people sitting around in a circle. Remind the group that this is a sign of God's presence. Play some quiet music in the background.

FOCUS ON FRIENDSHIP

Read by someone in the group.

Masie looked bleary-eyed and miserable. At break time she hardly spoke to anyone. In class she was miles away, just gazing into space. Even the teacher noticed. When he told her to "Wake up for goodness' sake and get on with your work," she jumped up and ran out of the room in tears.

When I next saw her she was sitting on a bench in the park. I went and sat down next to her. She said her parents were rowing all the time, and talking about splitting up, and that she didn't want to go home because it was so stressful. She was so upset just talking about it set her off crying again.

At first I was at a loss how to help her, so I just put my arm around her and sat quietly with her while she sobbed. As we sat there I prayed for God's guidance. Then it occurred to me that she might want someone to walk home with every day, so she could face the situation at home.

APPLICATION

Sometimes it takes courage to speak to someone who doesn't seem okay, especially at school when we could just go off and have fun with our friends.

Sometimes it's hard to know how to be with someone who's upset, and we can feel at a loss for words. But if we pray with open hearts and wait for God's answer, God will always show us the best thing to do.

PRAYER

Pass around slips of paper and pens. Invite each of the young people to compose a prayer to place in a basket, which is then placed in the centre. Tell the group this is a time of quiet prayer and reflection, in which they may ask for God's direction in how to support someone in need, or how to ask someone for help if they are in need themselves.

Invite the group to say the following prayer together from their books:

CLOSING PRAYER

Father, pour out your Spirit

upon your young people,

and grant us

a new vision of your glory,

a new experience of your power,

a new faithfulness to your Word; and

a new consecration to your service,

that your love may grow in us,

and your kingdom come.

Through Christ our Lord.

Amen.

SOCIAL TIME

10-20 minutes.

RECORD SHEET

TRUE VALUES

ADULT COMPANION'S REFLECTION

What are the major influences in your life? Do the media, the internet and/or peer pressure play a part? In what way? It may be that your influences are very different to those experienced by young people.

This enquiry begins with an opportunity for a broad discussion about influences that affect young people's lives. Allow the young people to lead the enquiry and for the discussion to flow. Make them the experts — they know their lives in a way that no adult can.

At this stage in *Life*, your relationship with the young people will hopefully be getting to a point of trust. Gently question and encourage the group to explore the factors that influence them, rather than accepting things at face value.

Invite the group to be quiet. Offer each person an opportunity to name an intention (such as a name or situation). Bring all these together in saying a prayer:

PRAYER

Father, pour out your Holy Spirit upon us

your sons and daughters.

May we see with your eyes,

judge all things in your light

and act with love in our hearts.

Mould us into your apostles

full of joy and hope,

so that we can be the difference

and your kingdom come

and keep us under your protection.

Through Christ Jesus our friend and Saviour.

Amen.

There is an alternative prayer suggested in the last chapter of the young people's book:

PRAYER

Lord Jesus,

We thank you for this day.

We offer you all our hopes and struggles, joys and sorrows.

Help us to grow together in friendship,

so that our words and actions bear witness to you

and make a difference in people's lives.

We pray for our families, for those who are hungry, lonely, poor and homeless,

and for all who have asked for our prayers.

May you bless us with wisdom to care for the earth.

May you bless us in love to care for one another.

In your name may we make all things new.

Amen.

ICE-BREAKER – CELEBS

Use the following ice-breaker or another of your choice (a selection of alternatives can be found in the Appendices).

PREPARATION: Prepare labels with the name of a celebrity on each. The celebrities will be familiar to young people: a soap character, singing idol or film star. Ensure you have tape and paper available.

Attach a label to each young person's back without them knowing whose name is on it. The group should then split into pairs. The object of the game is that each person guesses who their celebrity is. To discover this they ask their partner questions to which the partner can only reply with "yes" or "no". When a correct guess has been made, the two swap roles. The winners are the pair who guess their celebs first.

NEWS ROUND

- What has happened to you this week?

- Share one fact from your week (a good or bad thing). What has made you think, caused you concern or given you reason to celebrate?

NOTE: If something significant comes up, it may be more important to follow it up than to complete today's enquiry. If you need to follow up on anything you can use the short enquiry approach found in the Appendices.

REVIEW

Invite the group to look at last week's record sheet or flipchart sheets. Ask the young people to share the results of their actions.

> Look back at the last time you met. Hold one another to account:
>
> - What individual or group actions did you decide upon?
>
> - Were these actions carried out?
>
> - If so, how did it go?

ENQUIRY

NOTE: If you complete an enquiry over several meetings, the Prayer, News Round and Review should be repeated at the beginning of each session.

ENQUIRY SUMMARY – SEE, JUDGE, ACT

Each enquiry has a central narrative, or flow, which can be summarised with a few questions. In each chapter we'll provide you with this summary to help you prepare and focus for your meetings:

SEE – How are we influenced by the media? How does it affect how we view ourselves?

JUDGE – What is the real value of each one of us?

ACT – How can we live positively in a world influenced by the media's judgements?

SEE

As you begin the session, encourage everyone to take notes in their book. Ask someone to take notes on the record sheet or flipchart paper so that everyone can see it.

Invite the young person who is leading the session to begin with the **SEE**, where the group will look at their real experience.

> - Who or what has the most influence on you?
>
> - How do TV, the media, the internet or peer pressure influence you?

Help the group to choose at least one aspect of the media to look at. All these aspects could be dealt with in turn depending on the interest of the group. You may need to extend the enquiry over several weeks.

> - TV
> - The internet
> - News
> - Music
> - Magazines
> - Fashion

TV

> - What do you watch on TV? How much time do you spend watching each day?
>
> - Do you have a TV in your room? Do you watch TV with your family?
>
> - Does the behaviour of young people in TV programmes reflect how young people are today? Why are young people presented in this way?
>
> - Do young people treat TV characters as role models? How does this impact their actions?
>
> - How do you think TV influences adults' views of young people?
>
> - How do you think TV influences young people's views of adults?

Technology is just a tool. In terms of getting the kids working together and motivating them, the teacher is the most important.

Bill Gates

THE INTERNET

> - How do you access the internet?
>
> - What do you use the internet for – for gaming, social networking, music, shopping, watching videos, homework?
>
> - How much time do you spend on different activities online? Have you or has anyone you know ever been or felt "addicted" to spending time on the internet?
>
> - Do you use social networking to message your friends on a regular basis?

NEWS

> - Do you read, watch and/or listen to the news? If so, why? If not, why not?
>
> - How does the news affect how you live your life? Why is that?

- What images of young people are presented in the news? What effect does this have on young people?

- How does the news influence adults' views of young people?

MUSIC AND MAGAZINES

- How much time do you spend listening to music? How do you listen to music?

- What influence does music have in your life? What influence do you think music has on other young people?

- What magazines do you read? How much time and money do you spend on magazines?

- What images of young people do magazines and music present?

- Do you feel pressured by music or magazines to live in a certain way? If so, how do they influence you?

JUDGE

This is the time when the young people explore what they think about these issues, what's good or bad about the situations, and what their faith says.

TV

- How does TV add quality to your life?

- In what ways can TV have a harmful effect on yourself and your family life? Think about the use of your time and the development of your attitudes and beliefs.

- In what ways can TV have a good effect in these areas?

I think it's brought the world a lot closer together, and will continue to do that. There are downsides to everything; there are unintended consequences to everything. The most corrosive piece of technology that I've ever seen is called television – but then, again, television, at its best, is magnificent.

Steve Jobs, founder of Apple

THE INTERNET

The internet has been a boon and a curse for teenagers.

J.K. Rowling, author

- What are some of the good things about the internet? When can the internet be a "curse" for you?

- Look at your Circle of Influence. Are any of your friends or contacts affected negatively by the internet?

- What is attractive about communicating with others over the internet? When does social networking or texting cause problems? How is it a problem?

NEWS

Today, the news is scandals; that is news, but the many children who don't have food – that's not news. This is grave. We can't rest easy while things are this way.

Pope Francis

- Is the news media a good thing? How should we react to the news?

- How should the news be? What would be a fair way for the news media to portray young people?

- What do you think might encourage more young people to engage with the news?

MUSIC AND MAGAZINES

I've always treated the music business as a business.

Simon Cowell, music producer

In the music business, I found it was much more about interviews, photo shoots and appearances rather than actual performing, which I do best.

Gareth Gates, singer

- What do you think is good and bad about music and magazines today?

GOSPEL ENQUIRY

Invite a young person (who should have had a chance to prepare) to read the Gospel passage aloud. Ask the group to listen carefully to the story and think about the time, place and people involved.

Time allowing, it can be a good idea to invite a second young person to re-read the passage, although again ensure that she or he has also had a chance to prepare it.

MATTHEW 6:24-34

No one can serve two masters; for a slave will either hate the one and love the other, or be devoted to the one and despise the other. You cannot serve God and wealth. Therefore I tell you, do not worry about your life, what you will eat or what you will drink, or about your body, what you will wear. Is not life more than food, and the body more than clothing? Look at the birds of the air; they neither sow nor reap nor gather into barns, and yet your heavenly Father feeds them. Are you not of more value than they? And can any of you by worrying add a single hour to your span of life? And why do you worry about clothing? Consider the lilies of the field, how they grow; they neither toil nor spin, yet I tell you, even Solomon in all his glory was not clothed like one of these. But if God so clothes the grass of the field, which is alive today and tomorrow is thrown into the oven, will he not much more clothe you – you of little faith? Therefore do not worry, saying, "What will we eat?" or "What will we drink?" or "What will we wear?" For it is the Gentiles who strive for all these things; and indeed your heavenly Father knows that you need all these things. But strive first for the kingdom of God and his righteousness, and all these things will be given to you as well. So do not worry about tomorrow, for tomorrow will bring worries of its own. Today's trouble is enough for today.

- Who is in this story and what happened?

- What was said? How do you think the people present would have reacted? Why?

The master in the story to whom Jesus refers could be many different things: money, success, worldly beauty, fame, popularity.

We all know that many companies and media outlets are interested only in getting us to buy their products. Marketing professionals earn a fortune by presenting us with airbrushed, touched-up images of perfect-looking people apparently living perfect lives.

We also all know that these images are a far cry from reality. But even though we know that peace and happiness don't come through acquiring that must-have gadget or the latest look, time and again we fall for the hype. There's nothing wrong

with taking care of our appearance, or buying something we want and need, but it so easily tips over into vanity or compulsive spending – something we do to keep up with other people.

- If we let these things influence us above everything else how does it affect our relationships with other people and God?

- Are you really aware how special you are to God? What does this mean about how we should act in the world?

- Do you think the message of this Gospel story is hard to live up to? Why?

ACT

Jesus answered them, "Beware that no one leads you astray".

Matthew 24:4

By committing to take action after we finish our enquiry we are saying that we want to make a difference in our lives and the lives of others. We are committing to live as disciples of Jesus.

In each chapter we will consider action in three categories:

HELP – Helping others through service.

TELL IT – Making others aware of what we have discovered.

STAND UP – Standing up on behalf of others who do not or cannot speak out for themselves.

As a group, think about a specific situation – probably from something you have been discussing today – which causes you concern. Could you – either as a group or as individuals – do anything to **HELP**, **TELL IT** or **STAND UP**?

HELP

This is about helping and supporting other people, and deepening our relationships.

Everyone has inside of him a piece of good news. The good news is that you don't know how great you can be! How much you can love! What you can accomplish! And what your potential is!

Anne Frank, diarist and writer, and holocaust victim

Become more aware of advertisements, images and portrayals of people and lifestyles in the media all around you:

- What is really being presented to you?

- What is being sold or held up as an example?

- How should you respond?

You could for example:

- Be more open to important news and issues in the media.

- Take positive inspiration from the media and learn about people suffering, either in this country or abroad. How could you help? What might you do to make a start?

TELL IT

This is about raising awareness, or drawing people's attention to something they should be aware of. You could for example:

- Speak to other young people about the importance of viewing the media with intelligence! Do not believe everything you read in the papers and watch on television.

- Does your parish have a website? Is there a section devoted to young people? What can you do to help?

STAND UP

This is about standing up for yourself, or on behalf of others who do not or cannot speak out for themselves.

Stand up for yourself:

- Spend less time watching TV in your room, on the internet or social networking. How could you better use your time with your family?

- As a customer you have "purchasing power" so choose your purchases carefully. Review which magazines and newspapers you buy. Do these present young people in a positive light? Are they truthful? If not, choose to buy something else.

Stand up on behalf of others:

- Stand up for the truth of how many good young people there are in your community.

- Write a press release for your local paper with a positive story about young people.

- Produce a film of young people's news. Where can you show it?

Invite the young people to commit to taking an action and to sharing their commitment with the group.

What action or actions have you committed to? How are you going to make a start?

The actions should be noted on the flipchart or record sheet. You will need to keep these notes safe to enable the group to look back next time to check what action has been carried out and to give continuity to the meetings.

REACH OUT AND LIVE LIFE!

Help the group to identify where they can make a difference.

Where can you make a difference as a group? Make a note to return to in Chapter Eight:

- Has this enquiry given you any ideas for your group project?

- Make a note in your book – ideas for group project.

- As individuals, commit to think and pray about your group project between now and the next session.

Invite the young people to give thought and prayer to the group project in the time between now and the next session.

NOTES

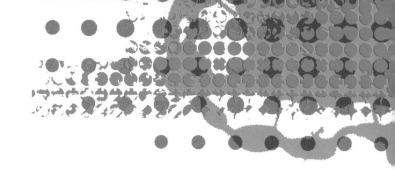

PRAYER TIME

PREPARATION: This prayer time requires some preparation to help the young people see how we can link the media to our prayer life. Find a newspaper article about a situation in the world which inspires prayer. In could be a story about people in need, or a story that requires more reflective thinking and praying about. In this example we've imagined using an article (perhaps from a Sunday feature) about clothes produced for the UK being made by young people overseas. Find some real facts to bring the story to life. A few minutes on an internet search engine will help, but choose the facts from a reputable charity, NGO or government department.

Light a candle in the middle of the room, with the young people sitting around in a circle. Remind the group that this is a sign of God's presence. Play some quiet music in the background.

SEEING IT AS IT IS

Read by someone in the group.

Ask a young person to read the article (or part of the article). Present some up-to-date facts, read by someone in the group. For example:

- 150 million children worldwide are in child labour.

- In the poorest countries in the world one in four children work in conditions bad for their health and well-being.

APPLICATION

We can use the media to help us find out about the needs of the world, but we shouldn't always take things at face value. Sometimes we might need to challenge what is being said to us, and check out the facts. At other times we might need to go a bit deeper, to discover the real situation behind the news story and find out how we can help. We should reflect on influences and make our own choices about how to respond.

There is always something we can do, even in the most challenging situations. Of course, sometimes we can't change the bigger picture, but using our **SEE, JUDGE, ACT** method, we can look deeper and discover the smaller changes we can make. For example, when considering child workers, how can we adjust our own spending habits? And when we can't see any way to make a difference, don't forget that we can pray.

PRAYER

Pass around slips of paper and pens. Invite each of the young people to compose a prayer to place in a basket, which is then placed in the centre. Tell the group this is a time of quiet prayer and reflection, in which they may ask for God's direction in how to support someone in need, or how to ask someone for help if they are in need themselves.

Invite the group to say the following prayer together from their books:

CLOSING PRAYER

Father, pour out your Spirit

upon your young people,

and grant us

a new vision of your glory,

a new experience of your power,

a new faithfulness to your Word; and

a new consecration to your service,

that your love may grow in us,

and your kingdom come.

Through Christ our Lord.

Amen.

SOCIAL TIME

10-20 minutes.

RECORD SHEET

4

UP CLOSE AND PERSONAL- IN TOUCH WITH GOD

ADULT COMPANION'S REFLECTION

Sometimes help comes from those closest to us who know us very well. At other times we turn to people who don't know us at all, as we need someone else to talk to. Consider when you have not been able to tell your nearest and dearest something, perhaps out of embarrassment or shame, but you have been able to admit things to a friend of a friend, or a colleague. We all need support, and we find it in different places at different times.

God can bring all of this together. God knows us better than we know ourselves, offering us a deep friendship. But we can also confide in God in ways that we can talk to no one else – admitting our secrets, owning up to our deepest fears and sharing our wildest ambitions.

Use this enquiry to help the young people explore a deeper relationship with God, especially through prayer and the Mass, so that they come to understand that God provides love and guidance in all aspects of their lives.

Invite the group to be quiet. Offer each person an opportunity to name an intention (such as a name or situation). Bring all these together in saying a prayer:

PRAYER

Lord Jesus,

Father, pour out your Holy Spirit upon us

your sons and daughters.

May we see with your eyes,

judge all things in your light

and act with love in our hearts.

Mould us into your apostles

full of joy and hope,

so that we can be the difference

and your kingdom come

and keep us under your protection.

Through Christ Jesus our friend and Saviour.

Amen.

There is an alternative prayer suggested in the last chapter of the young people's book:

PRAYER

We thank you for this day.

We offer you all our hopes and struggles, joys and sorrows.

Help us to grow together in friendship,

so that our words and actions bear witness to you

and make a difference in people's lives.

We pray for our families, for those who are hungry, lonely, poor and homeless,

and for all who have asked for our prayers.

May you bless us with wisdom to care for the earth.

May you bless us in love to care for one another.

In your name may we make all things new.

Amen.

ICE-BREAKER – UNTANGLE

Use the following ice-breaker, or another of your choice (a selection of alternatives can be found in the Appendices).

Ask everyone to stand in a circle, close together. Invite each person to put a hand in the middle of the circle and then to grasp someone else's hand, creating a tangle. Then ask everyone to grasp a different person's hand.

Tell the group that you would like them to untangle themselves without letting go of one another's hands. It is possible to untangle the circle, no matter how tangled it might seem (sometimes it unravels into more than one interlocking circle). People can change their grip to be a bit more comfortable, but they are not to cheat by letting go and re-clasping hands.

It may take some time at first, but usually it begins to speed up. Don't let the group give up. If it takes more than ten minutes, you may want to permit them one unclasp and re-clasp to help them along. They'll have to work together to decide how to use their one helping hand.

TIP

This works best with between seven and twelve people.

NEWS ROUND

- What has happened to you this week?

- Share one fact from your week (a good or bad thing). What has made you think, caused you concern or given you reason to celebrate?

NOTE: If something significant comes up, it may be more important to follow it up than to complete today's enquiry. If you need to follow up on anything you can use the short enquiry approach found in the Appendices.

REVIEW

Invite the group to look at last week's record sheet or flipchart sheets. Ask the young people to share the results of their actions.

Look back at the last time you met. Hold one another to account:

- What individual or group actions did you decide upon?

- Were these actions carried out?

- If so, how did it go?

ENQUIRY

NOTE: If you complete an enquiry over several meetings, the Prayer, News Round and Review should be repeated at the beginning of each session.

ENQUIRY SUMMARY – SEE, JUDGE, ACT

Each enquiry has a central narrative, or flow, which can be summarised with a few questions. In each chapter we'll provide you with this summary to help you prepare and focus for your meetings:

SEE – Where do we find support?

JUDGE – How does our faith support us?

ACT – What can we do to find more comfort and support in our relationship with God?

SEE

As you begin the session, encourage everyone to take notes in their book. Ask someone to take notes on the record sheet or flipchart paper so that everyone can see it.

Invite the young person who is leading the session to begin with the **SEE**, where the group will look at their real experience.

- Who do you turn to when you need help?

- Who are the really good friends you would turn to for support when you need it?

- Have you ever found help and support in an unlikely place or from someone you wouldn't expect it from?

NOTES

GETTING PERSONAL

Sometimes we face things in life that only those who know us really well can help with. But there are times, perhaps when we need to be really honest about ourselves or admit we need help to sort something out, when it's best to confide in someone we don't know so well, or a professional.

- Are there things you find difficult to talk about face to face with your best friends or family? Why? What kind of issues do you find it difficult to speak about?

- Where can you find help if you did not feel able to talk to your friends and family?

- Would you count God among those you can turn to? If not, why not?

JUDGE

This is the time when the young people explore what they think about these issues, what's good or bad about the situations, and what their faith says.

JASON'S STORY

Jason is sixteen. He is very popular at school, among his friends and his teachers. He's good at sport, drama, and study, and many people think he has the perfect life with a well-off family to match his talents. But Jason is struggling to find help with his family situation. His parents are arguing all the time and he is beginning to blame himself for not being able to help. Jason doesn't want to talk to anyone at school because he relies on his popularity so much and he doesn't want people to know that everything is not as good as they think it is.

He just wants to get away from it all, so he goes with a friend for a few days to house-sit for a relative. Instead of just forgetting about his family worries, he manages to get things in perspective and talk with his friend. His friend helps him to realise that nothing is his fault and that his family sounds like it is experiencing normal family difficulties. He encourages Jason to talk to the school chaplain. The chaplain helps him to realise that you don't always need to "get away" from things. Jason now takes time each day to talk to God. He says he finds comfort in finding that time of quiet every day.

- *Have you ever been in a similar situation?*

- *Turn back to Chapter Two and have a look at the Circle of Influence you drew. Think about who you know, who might have faced a situation like this.*

God's love for us is absolute. God's love won't change, even when we feel everything is going wrong. He is always there to support and guide us, and provide us with everything we need – even if at times it doesn't feel that way.

Therefore do not worry, saying, "What will we eat?" or "What will we drink?" or "What will we wear?"... indeed your heavenly Father knows that you need all these things.

Matthew 6:31-32

- Do you pray? When? Have you ever been aware of God helping you or guiding you?

- Do you find it easy to tell God everything?

- Can it sometimes be hard to pray? What obstacles might there be in talking to God?

There are different ways we can grow in our relationship with God. It's not just about asking God for what we want and need – we can also take time to pray prayers of thanks, praise and sorrow.

- When have you thanked or praised your friends of family for being part of your life?

- When have you said sorry? Why is it important?

- Can you see why this might be important for your relationship with God?

A SUNDAY INVITATION

We can also build our relationship with God by going to Mass. Sometimes we can think that going to Mass on a Sunday is just something expected of us, but in fact it is an invitation.

BREAKING NEWS

PACK YOUR BAGS, WE'RE OFF TO... CHURCH

Fr Michael Sonas says that going to Mass is like going on holiday and everyone is invited. He is planning to launch a new advertising campaign designed to reach out to the local community.

Mass can give us the chance to sort out what's really important. We can get things in perspective. It gives us the opportunity to meet Jesus in different ways: in listening to his word, in Holy Communion and in the people we meet. You might have heard people describe a holiday as a way of "recharging the batteries" – and Mass can do something similar. As we leave the church we are renewed and refreshed – ready to take on whatever comes our way.

- Where do you go or what do you do to "get away from it all"?

- Have you ever experienced the Mass as a holiday? Did you come out with a sense of having been refreshed, with a new perspective?

NOTES

Going to Mass makes me feel part of the community through singing and meeting others in the congregation. The Mass to me means the most powerful prayer and a time to have a conversation with God.

Marie, London

GOSPEL ENQUIRY

Invite a young person (who should have had a chance to prepare) to read the Gospel passage aloud. Ask the group to listen carefully to the story and think about the time, place and people involved.

Time allowing, it can be a good idea to invite a second young person to re-read the passage, although again ensure that she or he has had a chance to prepare it.

JOHN 21:2-14

Gathered there together were Simon Peter, Thomas called the Twin, Nathanael of Cana in Galilee, the sons of Zebedee, and two others of his disciples. Simon Peter said to them, "I am going fishing." They said to him, "We will go with you." They went out and got into the boat, but that night they caught nothing. Just after daybreak, Jesus stood on the beach; but the disciples did not know that it was Jesus. Jesus said to them, "Children, you have no fish, have you?" They answered him, "No." He said to them, "Cast the net to the right side of the boat, and you will find some." So they cast it, and now they were not able to haul it in because there were so many fish. That disciple whom Jesus loved said to Peter, "It is the Lord!" When Simon Peter heard that it was the Lord, he put on some clothes, for he was naked, and jumped into the sea. But the other disciples came in the boat, dragging the net full of fish, for they were not far from the land, only about a hundred yards off. When they had gone ashore, they saw a charcoal fire there, with fish on it, and bread. Jesus said to them, "Bring some of the fish that you have just caught." So Simon Peter went aboard and hauled the net ashore, full of large fish, a hundred fifty-three of them; and though there were so many, the net was not torn. Jesus said to them, "Come and have breakfast." Now none of the disciples dared to ask him, "Who are you?" because they knew it was the Lord. Jesus came and took the bread and gave it to them, and did the same with the fish. This was now the third time that Jesus appeared to the disciples after he was raised from the dead.

- Who is in this story and what happened?

- What was said? How do you think the people present would have reacted? Why?

The story gives us a wonderful example of how Jesus comes to the aid of his friends.

The disciples were in need, struggling to catch any fish. If this had continued, they would have had no fish to eat or sell to earn their living. Jesus came to them and, although they didn't recognise him, he offered his advice. After listening to him and acting upon his words, some of the disciples realised who he was. They brought their catch of fish to him, and in sitting with him around the fire sharing the bread he offered, all the disciples now recognised him.

- Have you ever been aware of God helping you, even before asking him?

- Jesus asked the disciples to bring the results of their work to him. We are encouraged to offer the fruits of our lives to God every Sunday when we go to Mass. What "fruits" can you bring to offer God?

- Where do you recognise God helping you in life?

ACT

By committing to take action after we finish our enquiry we are saying that we want to make a difference in our lives and the lives of others. We are committing to living as disciples of Jesus.

Whenever you pray, go into your room and shut the door and pray to your Father who is in secret; and your Father who sees in secret will reward you.

Matthew 6:6

In each chapter we will consider action in three categories:

HELP – *Helping others through service.*

TELL IT – *Making others aware of what we have discovered.*

STAND UP – *Standing up on behalf of others who do not or cannot speak out for themselves.*

As a group, think about a specific situation – probably from something you have been discussing today – which causes you concern. Could you – either as a group or as individuals – do anything to **HELP**, **TELL IT** or **STAND UP**?

HELP

This is about helping and supporting other people, and deepening our relationships.

REVIEW OF THE DAY

Discuss with the young people the importance of ending each day with God. In their books they have the following guide to complete a Review of the Day. Encourage the young people to use this each evening:

We are called to follow God in each moment of every day. Review your day before you go to bed:

- What has happened today? Who did I meet?

- How have I responded to God's call today?

- Did I bring God's love into each moment?

This can lead to:

- Thanking God – for the good things that happened today.

- Being sorry – for those actions, words and thoughts which have come between

you and others, and you and God.

- Petition – asking God for your own needs and the needs of others.

- Appreciating how wonderful God is, and expressing it in prayer.

MASS

Encourage the group to think about their participation in the Mass, and how they can develop their relationship with God. (There are resources listed in the Appendices to help with this.)

- Go to Mass when you normally wouldn't (for example, during the week). Take special notice of the different parts of the Mass.

Help other people through service:

- Look at your Circle of Influence. Who can you pray for?

- Did you commit to a parish role within the Mass? How is it going?

TELL IT

This is about raising awareness, or drawing people's attention to something they should be aware of:

- Can you help one another to become more aware of prayer and the Mass? How?

- Is there anyone you can invite to speak to your group to help you understand the Mass further, and how we can take part more fully?

- Could you put something in the parish newsletter from our enquiry today to encourage young people to think about the Mass more and how to pray?

STAND UP

This is about standing up for yourself, or on behalf of others who do not or cannot speak out for themselves. You might decide to:

- Be prepared to say that you go to Mass to your friends.

- Not stand quietly by if you see anyone being victimised because of their beliefs.

Invite the young people to commit to taking an action and to sharing their commitment with the group.

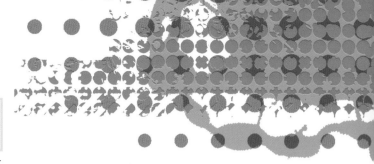

> What action or actions have you committed to? How are you going to make a start?

The actions should be noted on the flipchart or record sheet. You will need to keep these notes safe to enable the group to look back next time to check what action has been carried out and to give continuity to the meetings.

REACH OUT AND LIVE LIFE!

Help the group to identify where they can make a difference.

> Where can you make a difference as a group? Make a note to return to in Chapter Eight:
>
> * Has this enquiry given you any ideas for your group project?
>
> * Make a note in your book – ideas for group project.
>
> * As individuals, commit to think and pray about your group project between now and the next session.

Invite the young people to give thought and prayer to the group project in the time between now and the next session.

PRAYER TIME

Light a candle in the middle of the room, with the young people sitting around in a circle. Remind the group that this is a sign of God's presence. Play some quiet music in the background.

BEING PEOPLE OF PRAYER

Read by someone in the group.

> **JESUS IS ONLY A PRAYER AWAY**
>
> *Above all Jesus loves us and wants us to talk to him from our hearts, as we would to our best friend. To express those inner yearnings, to share our day with him, to ask for help. We can talk with him anywhere, even on the bus and somehow he talks to us, we have a sense of what he is be saying. He is with us in every situation, just a prayer away.*

APPLICATION

Formal set prayers are good when said with reverence and sincerity, especially when said with others at Mass or in some other setting with a group. At the same time Jesus is looking for a personal conversation with each one of us because he loves each of us individually.

PRAYER

Pass around slips of paper and pens. Invite each of the young people to compose a prayer to place in a basket, which is then placed in the centre. Tell the group this is a time of quiet prayer and reflection, in which they may ask for God's direction in how to support someone in need, or how to ask someone for help if they are in need themselves.

Invite the group to say the following prayer together from their books:

> **CLOSING PRAYER**
>
> Father, pour out your Spirit
>
> upon your young people,
>
> and grant us
>
> a new vision of your glory,
>
> a new experience of your power,
>
> a new faithfulness to your Word; and
>
> a new consecration to your service,
>
> that your love may grow in us,
>
> and your kingdom come.
>
> Through Christ our Lord.
>
> Amen.

SOCIAL TIME

10-20 minutes.

RECORD SHEET

RELATIONSHIPS, SEX AND ALL THAT

ADULT COMPANION'S REFLECTION

This session about love and sexual relationships deliberately has its reference point as the Catholic Church's view of Christian marriage. It does not, however, set out to preach to the young people, but rather to invite them to explore their own experience and that of their peers, and then to consider why the Church teaches what it does about love and relationships and how this teaching can support them.

Obviously it needs careful handling with this age group, and from the outset it should be made clear that nobody needs to talk about anything they are not comfortable discussing, and confidentiality should be respected at all times. For example, people should be free to discuss real-life situations, but naming names should be avoided.

There are some possible pitfalls and you, as the adult companion, may feel the need to tell the young people what is best for them, or to lay Church teaching on the line. However, it is best if the young people are encouraged to answer the questions and speak freely. The principle involved here, as in all the sessions, is to start from where the young people are. There may be situations discussed which relate specifically to the first-hand experience of young people or their family and friends. Care should be taken here that no judgements are made.

The age group of the young people will determine what kind of relationships they talk about. Young people may want to talk about other issues, for example same-sex relationships. Although this session touches on this topic, it does not exhaust it. However, do not be tempted to end the discussion, but link it back to the session contents, encouraging the group to consider why the Church teaches what it does about love and relationships, and to explore the goodness of the teaching, as well as the challenges.

There are other topics which may come up, not explicitly dealt with here. Perhaps the most significant is abortion. It would be impossible to properly deal with this issue in this chapter, so there is an enquiry on abortion in the Appendices, which can help to facilitate proper enquiry into this important issue if it comes up.

PREPARATION: Take magazines along with you for the "Sex Sells" section.

Invite the group to be quiet. Offer each person an opportunity to name an intention (such as a name or situation). Bring all these together in saying a prayer:

PRAYER

 Father, pour out your Holy Spirit upon us

your sons and daughters.

May we see with your eyes,

judge all things in your light

and act with love in our hearts.

Mould us into your apostles

full of joy and hope,

so that we can be the difference

and your kingdom come

and keep us under your protection.

Through Christ Jesus our friend and Saviour.

Amen.

There is an alternative prayer suggested in the last chapter of the young people's book:

PRAYER

Lord Jesus,

We thank you for this day.

We offer you all our hopes and struggles, joys and sorrows.

Help us to grow together in friendship,

so that our words and actions bear witness to you

and make a difference in people's lives.

We pray for our families, for those who are hungry, lonely, poor and homeless,

and for all who have asked for our prayers.

May you bless us with wisdom to care for the earth.

May you bless us in love to care for one another.

In your name may we make all things new.

Amen.

ICE-BREAKER – GOTCHA!

Use the following ice-breaker, or another of your choice (a selection of alternatives can be found in the Appendices).

Ask the group to form a fairly tight circle, facing inwards. Each person then extends an open right hand with the palm flat and face up, and the person on their right places their left index finger across their neighbour's hand. The entire circle is thus joined in this way – open right hand and index finger in the palm of the person on their left.

The adult companion (or one of the young people) then counts to an unspecified number and in his/her own time calls "Gotcha!" very loudly. At this point everyone simultaneously closes their right hand to trap the index finger of the person on their right and snatches away their left index finger so as not to get caught by their neighbour.

In each round, those who succeed in both catching a finger and avoiding being caught form a smaller circle and repeat the exercise, until one person is the overall winner.

The rules are:

- The palm must be flat and finger must be straight.

- Anyone who anticipates the call is out.

NEWS ROUND

- What has happened to you this week?

- Share one fact from your week (a good or bad thing). What has made you think, caused you concern or given you reason to celebrate?

NOTE: If something significant comes up, it may be more important to follow it up than to complete today's enquiry. If you need to follow up on anything you can use the short enquiry approach found in the Appendices.

REVIEW

Invite the group to look at last week's record sheet or flipchart sheets. Ask the young people to share the results of their actions.

Look back at the last time you met. Hold one another to account:

- What individual or group actions did you decide upon?

- Were these actions carried out?

- If so, how did it go?

ENQUIRY

NOTE: If you complete an enquiry over several meetings, the Prayer, News Round and Review should be repeated at the beginning of each session.

ENQUIRY SUMMARY – SEE, JUDGE, ACT

Each enquiry has a central narrative, or flow, which can be summarised with a few questions. In each chapter we'll provide you with this summary to help you prepare and focus for your meetings:

SEE – How do young people experience sex and relationships?

JUDGE – What is God's wish for us in our relationships?

ACT – How can we build foundations for good relationships?

SEE

As you begin the session, encourage everyone to take notes in their book. Ask someone to take notes on the record sheet or flipchart paper so that everyone can see it.

Invite the young person who is leading the session to begin with the **SEE**, where the group will look at their real experience.

- Are you or any of your friends in a romantic relationship?

- How serious are the relationships?

- Do you think you will get married one day, or isn't it "on your radar"?

SEX SELLS

You've probably heard the expression "sex sells". Just open any glossy magazine, turn on the TV, or look at the ads down the side of a web page. That bang-on-trend pair of jeans, the must-have top, or the cool shoes – chances they caught your eye because of the gorgeous, sexy model wearing them.

But these images don't just sell us ideas of what to buy or wear – they also sell us ways to think and behave.

- What images of sexual and romantic relationships do young people meet on TV, in magazines, films and music?

- How does the way in which relationships are portrayed in the media influence the behaviour and attitudes of young people?

- Where do we get our idea about what love is? Make a list

- The Greeks had four words for love, these are:

  - *Agape*, for total giving

  - *Phileo*, for affection

  - *Eros*, for physical or sexual love, and

  - *Stergo*, for family love

- Which kind of love is depicted more in the media today?

JUDGE

This is the time when the young people explore what they think about these issues, what's good or bad about the situations, and what their faith says.

MARRIAGE – THE NEW TABOO?

God disposed man and woman for each other so that they might be "no longer two, but one" (Matthew 19:6). In this way they are to live in love, be fruitful, and thus become signs of God himself, who is nothing but overflowing love.

YouCat 260, from Catechism of the Catholic Church

- What do you think this means?

WHY WAIT?

"I love my boyfriend and it's not just that I fancy him. I really love just being with him so why shouldn't we have sex?" **Judith**

"I made some bad mistakes as a teenager and ended up regretting them. Now I wish I'd waited until I met the right person." **Dougie**

"I know that having sex should be making love. But sometimes it can be fun too. And besides, who says marriage is the only place where love can happen?" **Veronica**

"I had a couple of boyfriends at college and then when I got married I found I couldn't have children because I had caught chlamydia without knowing it and it wasn't treated." **Susan**

"I became pregnant in school year 11. I thought I loved my boyfriend at the time, but we're not together anymore. I love my baby boy though. I realise it is a big responsibility having a baby to look after. I am so happy my parents are supporting me. I don't know how I would be able to cope otherwise." **Sam**

- What do you think about these statements?

- Without naming names, have any of your friends been involved in early sexual relationships?

- Do you know anyone who became pregnant while still at school? What do we think of this?

- Do you think early sex is healthy? What do you think the drawbacks might be – physically, emotionally, socially?

- Why do you think the Church teaches that we should wait until marriage before having sex?

When a husband and wife make love, they are saying to each other: "I love you without reserve; I give you my whole self; I accept your gift of yourself to me; and together we are open to the gift of new life that may come from our love".

A Way of Life for Young Catholics, Fr Stephen Wang

- When young people have sex before marriage what are they saying to each other? In what ways could this be similar to a husband and wife making love? How is it different?

- Which of the four Greek words for love describes Christian marriage?

- Is it difficult to retain the idea of sexual love as something precious and special?

WHAT ABOUT PEOPLE WHO ARE GAY?

In 2013 Pope Francis made headlines around the world. He was on the plane back from celebrating Mass for three million young people at World Youth Day in Brazil when he was asked about people in the Church who are gay. He answered, "If a person is gay and seeks God and has good will, who am I to judge?"

In saying this, the Pope was not casting aside Church teaching on homosexual relationships and the centrality of love and marriage between a man and a woman, but he was emphasising that everyone is welcome, without judgment, in the family of the Church.

Christians owe all persons respect and love, ... regardless of their sexual orientation, because all people are respected and loved by God.

YouCat, 65

- What do you think about this?

- Do you know anyone who is gay? If so, do you think she or he feels included and welcome in the Church?

- How can we as a Church help gay people feel a real part of our community?

GOSPEL ENQUIRY

Invite a young person (who should have had a chance to prepare) to read the Gospel passage aloud. Ask the group to listen carefully to the story and think about the time, place and people involved.

Time allowing, it can be a good idea to invite a second young person to re-read the passage, although again ensure that she or he has also had a chance to prepare it.

MARK 10:2-8

Some Pharisees came, and to test him they asked, "Is it lawful for a man to divorce his wife?" He answered them, "What did Moses command you?" They said, "Moses allowed a man to write a certificate of dismissal and to divorce her." But Jesus said to them, "Because of your hardness of heart he wrote this commandment for you. 'But from the beginning of creation, God made them male and female. For this reason a man shall leave his father and mother and be joined to his wife, and the two shall become one flesh.' So they are no longer two, but one flesh."

- Who is in this story and what happened?

- What was said? How do you think the people present would have reacted? Why?

Although many young people in the group will have witnessed marriage lived out within their families, and sadly some will have witnessed divorce too, marriage is not likely to be on their radar any time soon. However, this Gospel passage is not simply about marriage and divorce. The rare mention by Jesus of marriage points to an understanding of Christian love, which has timeless relevance for young people. In a world where sexuality is turned into a commodity, and freedom is confused with being a slave to non-stop choice, returning to a Christian understanding of commitment can be liberating for young people.

Our commitment to one another is not transient, whether in friendships, families or with the person we choose to spend our whole life with. God has a plan for us, from the beginning of creation, and we are invited by God to help to fulfil that plan. When we choose to be joined with another, to become one flesh with them, we are choosing to remain that way for the rest of our lives. This profound invitation is not a discipline to restrict, but a gift from God to live freely with another person who will help to fulfil us.

- What is Jesus saying to us in this passage?

- From this passage, what view of relationships do you think God has?

- What is meant by, "no longer two, but one flesh"?

ACT

By committing ourselves to take action after we finish our enquiry we are saying that we want to make a difference in our lives and the lives of others. We are committing to living as disciples of Jesus.

- Do you think it possible and worthwhile to live with another person for the rest of your life?

In each chapter we will consider action in three categories:

HELP – Helping others through service.

TELL IT – Making others aware of what we have discovered.

STAND UP – Standing up on behalf of others who do not or cannot speak out for themselves.

As a group, think about a specific situation – probably from something you have been discussing today – which causes you concern. Could you, either as a group or as individuals, do anything to **HELP**, **TELL IT** or **STAND UP**?

HELP

This is about helping and supporting other people, and deepening our relationships.

- Look at your Circle of Influence and give thought and prayer to whether there is any way in which you could help a friend in relationship difficulties.

TELL IT

This is about raising awareness, or drawing people's attention to something they should be aware of. Young people could for example:

- Commit to finding out more about the Church's teaching. Where can you make a start?

- Be ready with facts and examples when discussing the issues which face young people when making lifestyle choices.

- If your views conflict with those of your friends, be prepared to be honest.

TIP

YouCat, the young people's version of the Catechism of the Catholic Church, is a good starting point for exploring the teaching of the Church. See Appendices for details.

STAND UP

This is about standing up for yourself, or on behalf of others who do not or cannot speak out for themselves. The young people might decide to:

- Write to a broadcasting authority about some of the issues in connection with the media you have discussed in **SEE**. How can you find out their contact details?

Invite the young people to commit to taking an action and to sharing their commitment with the group.

What action or actions have you committed to? How are you going to make a start?

The actions should be noted on the flipchart or record sheet. You will need to keep these notes safe to enable the group to look back next time to check what action has been carried out and to give continuity to the meetings.

REACH OUT AND LIVE LIFE!

Help the group to identify where they can make a difference.

Where can you make a difference as a group? Make a note to return to in Chapter Eight:

- Has this enquiry given you any ideas for your group project?

- Make a note in your book – ideas for group project.

- As individuals, commit to think and pray about your group project between now and the next session.

Invite the young people to give thought and prayer to the group project in the time between now and the next session.

NOTES

PRAYER TIME

Light a candle in the middle of the room with the young people sitting around in a circle. Remind the group that this is a sign of God's presence. Play some quiet music in the background.

GOD'S GRACE TO GET IT RIGHT

Read by someone in the group.

> *A short course on human relationships.*
>
> *The six most important words: I admit that I was wrong.*
>
> *The five most important words: You did a great job.*
>
> *The four most important words: What do you think?*
>
> *The three most important words: Could you please... ?*
>
> *The two most important words: Thank you.*
>
> *The most important word: We.*
>
> *The least important word: I.*
>
> **J.John & Mark Stibbe,**
> **"A Short Course in Human Relationships",**
> ***A Barrel of Fun* (2003: Monarch)**

APPLICATION

A successful relationship is just not about being with the right person but being the right partner. Although marriage is a far-off possibility for young people, successful lifelong relationships begin in the here and now. For this we need God's grace.

PRAYER

Pass around slips of paper and pens. Invite each of the young people to compose a prayer to place in a basket, which is then placed in the centre. Tell the group this is a time of quiet prayer and reflection, in which they may ask for God's direction in how to support someone in need, or how to ask someone for help if they are in need themselves.

Invite the group to say the following prayer together from their books:

CLOSING PRAYER

Father, pour out your Spirit

upon your young people,

and grant us

a new vision of your glory,

a new experience of your power,

a new faithfulness to your Word; and

a new consecration to your service,

that your love may grow in us,

and your kingdom come.

Through Christ our Lord.

Amen.

SOCIAL TIME

10-20 minutes.

RECORD SHEET

WHEN WE'RE STRUGGLING

ADULT COMPANION'S REFLECTION

Everyone, without exception, is in some way affected by mental health issues. It may be personal experience, or have affected our family, friends, colleagues or peer group. There is still, sadly, a taboo around mental health problems. Fear or misunderstanding can lead to people not seeking help, hiding the issues, or simply pretending there isn't a problem in the first place. With a quarter of us all likely to experience mental health problems in our lifetime, and at least one in ten young people suffering right now, it shouldn't be an issue we shy away from.

As a Church we are called to accompany our young people in all aspects of their lives, through their successes and challenges, to help them to grow into the people God has created them to be. In this chapter, we reflect on how God's glory is seen in each and every one of us being "fully alive". We can support our young people in discovering what this is, and offer them practical ways of caring for their own well-being and for others, so that they can bring God's glory into the world.

Invite the group to be quiet. Offer each person an opportunity to name an intention (such as a name or situation). Bring all these together in saying a prayer:

PRAYER

Father, pour out your Holy Spirit upon us your sons and daughters.

May we see with your eyes,

judge all things in your light

and act with love in our hearts.

Mould us into your apostles

full of joy and hope,

so that we can be the difference

and your kingdom come

and keep us under your protection.

Through Christ Jesus our friend and Saviour.

Amen.

There is an alternative prayer suggested in the last chapter of the young people's book:

PRAYER

Lord Jesus,

We thank you for this day.

We offer you all our hopes and struggles, joys and sorrows.

Help us to grow together in friendship,

so that our words and actions bear witness to you

and make a difference in people's lives.

We pray for our families, for those who are hungry, lonely, poor and homeless,

and for all who have asked for our prayers.

May you bless us with wisdom to care for the earth.

May you bless us in love to care for one another.

In your name may we make all things new.

Amen.

ICE-BREAKER – TRUST GAME

Use the following ice-breaker, or another of your choice (a selection of alternatives can be found in the Appendices).

This is the classic trust game, which works very well with any age group. It fits in to our theme in this chapter of trusting that things will be okay, and being there to help our friends.

Divide the group into pairs according to height and weight. (Of course this needs handling with discretion so that nobody is made to feel self-conscious.) Each pair decides who will "fall" and who will "catch" first. The one catching stands behind the other, allowing his or her partner to fall backwards. When both are ready, and when the catcher is paying careful attention, the partner being caught falls backward as a dead weight to be caught in the open arms of the catcher. It may take a couple of attempts before the faller has enough trust to go through with it. The couples then swap around.

Demonstrate it first, and keep, a careful eye on everyone, to ensure that they are taking it seriously and that no one is injured through carelessness or messing about.

NEWS ROUND

- What has happened to you this week?

- Share one fact from your week (a good or bad thing). What has made you think, caused you concern or given you reason to celebrate?

NOTE: If something significant comes up, it may be more important to follow it up than to complete today's enquiry. If you need to follow up on anything you can use the short enquiry approach found in the Appendices.

REVIEW

Invite the group to look at last week's record sheet or flipchart sheets. Ask the young people to share the results of their actions.

Look back at the last time you met. Hold one another to account:

- What individual or group actions did you decide upon?

- Were these actions carried out?

- If so, how did it go?

ENQUIRY

NOTE: If you complete an enquiry over several meetings, the Prayer, News Round and Review should be repeated at the beginning of each session.

ENQUIRY SUMMARY – SEE, JUDGE, ACT

Each enquiry has a central narrative, or flow, which can be summarised with a few questions. In each chapter we'll provide you with this summary to help you prepare and focus for your meetings:

SEE – How do mental health issues affect us and others who we know?

JUDGE – What does being fully alive mean?

ACT – How can we take care of our own well-being and support others?

SEE

As you begin the session, encourage everyone to take notes in their book. Ask someone to take notes on the record sheet or flipchart paper so that everyone can see it.

Invite the young person who is leading the session to begin with the **SEE**, where the group will look at their real experience.

WELL-BEING

To live a full life that makes a difference we need to look after ourselves. Unfortunately, there are many things that challenge the well-being of young people today – among them poor mental health. It is often not spoken about, but it affects at least one in ten young people. It can be devastating for individuals, families and friendships, leaving young people unable to live fulfilled lives.

- Do you, or any young people you know, experience mental health issues?

You are amazing young people and I want you to make the most of your lives and to make wise choices. Many of you will have mental health problems or know someone who has. Mental illness is very common in young people. There are some things that can make you ill, but there are ways we can keep well.

Baroness Sheila Hollins, speaking at Flame 2, March 2015, Wembley Arena

What can hurt our minds? In her address at Flame, Baroness Hollins identified five things that spell **ABUSE**:

Addiction – to food, alcohol, drugs, sex, porn, the internet, your smartphone.

Boredom – leads to seeking out unhealthy means of fulfilment.

Used – if you are bullied, abused, feeling powerless. **It's not your fault**.

Solo – if you are feeling alone, rejected, or grieving.

Excluded – if you are on the outside of the group, different in some way.

Her advice was to "Avoid **ABUSE**" – if you notice these things happening, speak to someone. If you notice a friend don't judge them, don't ignore them, reach out to them.

- When have you experienced any of these five elements of **ABUSE**?

- Does anyone you know in your Circle of Influence chart have any similar difficulties?

- How do these issues affect our friends, family and day-to-day life?

Baroness Hollins went on to ask, "What can we do to look after ourselves?" The answer, she said, is to live in **GRACE**:

Give something – your time, your prayer, something you made.

Receive – be loved, love yourself and then love others. It's hard to love someone else unless you learn to be loved yourself.

Active – swim, run, dance – it's difficult to be depressed when you are on the move.

Create – learn something new every day, make something – art, music. Enjoy God's creation.

Engage – with life and with people in the real world. You can't hug a computer! But we all need a hug every day.

Finally, she urged her young listeners to "Do **GRACE** every day. These five things are proven to help you stay healthy."

- Do you do any of these things every day?

- Which ones do you find most of a challenge?

JUDGE

This is the time when the young people explore what they think about these issues, what's good or bad about certain situations, and what their faith says.

The responsibility to look after ourselves in body, mind and spirit, comes from the unimaginable reality that we are made in the image and likeness of God. God chose to make us like him! So to lead full lives we are called to take care of ourselves, and to take care of others, so that God's likeness in us can be celebrated.

The glory of God is a human being fully alive.
St Irenaeus

- What does this mean?

- What does it mean for how we live our lives in the service of others?

NOTES

BECKY'S STORY

Becky was fifteen when the stress and pressure of life resulted in her getting depressed. School was too much for her. No matter how hard she tried, she couldn't keep up with the coursework. Home was too much for her. Her mum had been unwell for a long time, but unwilling to admit it, so things were now difficult between her mum and dad. And her love life was too much for her. Or, rather, the lack of it. The boy she loved was not interested. So she found herself trapped in her own world. She thought nobody would understand and she withdrew into her bedroom. Things just got worse. One day she started self-harming. She cut deep lines into her arms and burned herself deliberately. She didn't know why she did it, but it seemed to relive the tension within her.

One day, at school, her friend Jack asked her what was wrong. He was the first person to actually ask her about it. So, for some reason, she told him everything. It helped Becky to see that there were good things in life, and that maybe getting help might be worth it. With support from the school counsellor, she got the help she needed.

Once Becky was feeling better and living life fully again, she was able to help her mum and things started to improve at home.

- *How important was it that Jack asked Becky how she was and, helped by someone else, she could go on and help her family?*

- *Who do you know who might need the loving concern and friendship that Jack showed Becky?*

GOSPEL ENQUIRY

Invite a young person (who should have had a chance to prepare) to read the Gospel passage aloud. Ask the group to listen carefully to the story and think about the time, place and people involved.

Time allowing, it can be a good idea to invite a second young person to re-read the passage, although again ensure that she or he has also had a chance to prepare it.

JOHN 14:1-6

"Do not let your hearts be troubled. Believe in God, believe also in me. In my Father's house there are many dwelling places. If it were not so, would I have told you that I go to prepare a place for you? And if I go and prepare a place for you, I will come again and will take you to myself, so that where I am, there you may be also. And you know the way to the place where I am going." Thomas said to him, "Lord, we do not know where you are going. How can we know the way?" Jesus said to him, "I am the way, and the truth, and the life."

- Who is in this story and what happened?

- What was said? How do you think the people present would have reacted? Why?

Jesus invites his disciples to "believe" in him. He will not forget them but is preparing a place for them. No matter what the world might throw at the disciples, he is giving them a vision of the future, and he is inviting them to trust him, that everything will be ok. In the midst of challenges of teenage years, for many further impacted by anxiety, pressure and poor mental health, it can be difficult to trust that things will get better.

In this Gospel story Jesus offers hope for the future. He promises to be there always – "Where I am, there you may be also". It is a story of God's love for us. It is also an example of Jesus' commitment and comfort towards his friends. No matter how bad life can get, we can offer hope to our friends and we can find hope and comfort in Jesus.

- Can you relate the story to the situations you have been looking at?

- Is there anyone you feel called to help, who may be struggling with their mental well-being?

ACT

Peace I leave with you; my peace I give to you. I do not give to you as the world gives. Do not let your hearts be troubled, and do not let them be afraid.

John 14:27

By committing ourselves to take action after we finish our enquiry we are saying that we want to make a difference in our lives and the lives of others. We are committing to live as disciples of Jesus.

In each chapter we will consider action in three categories:

HELP – Helping others through service.

TELL IT – Making others aware of what we have discovered.

STAND UP – Standing up on behalf of others who do not or cannot speak out for themselves.

As a group, think about a specific situation – probably from something you have been discussing today – which causes you concern. Could you – either as a group or as individuals – do anything to **HELP**, **TELL IT** or **STAND UP**?

HELP

This is about helping and supporting yourself and other people, and deepening relationships:

- How could you avoid **ABUSE** and live in **GRACE** this week?

- Look at your Circle of Influence Chart and give thought and prayer to whether there is any way in which you could help a friend in a difficult situation.

- Do you know anyone suffering from mental health issues? How can you show your support for them?

SUPPORTING OTHERS WITH MENTAL HEALTH PROBLEMS

Examples of how to help others with stressful situations:

- *Don't avoid them because you don't know what to say. Show that you care by giving your time and listening to them. Be patient and go on listening even when they seem to be going round in circles.*

- *Be ready to help them practically. Sometimes for smallest things, like accompanying someone to an appointment, can make all the difference. Offer ideas about doing fun things together to help them relax.*

- *If someone needs to see the doctor there is nothing for them to be embarrassed about. Stick by them and offer support.*

TELL IT

This is about raising awareness, or drawing people's attention to something they should be aware of. You could for example:

- Encourage people to get involved in supporting others.

- Raise awareness about mental health issues. Search online for mental health awareness campaigns near you.

- Tell others about places they can get support, especially those who experience mental health issues.

NOTES

ChildLine – a private and confidential service for children and young people up to the age of nineteen: **www.childline. org.uk**

Young Minds – committed to improving the emotional well-being and mental health of children and young people: **www.youngminds.org.uk**

Young Carers – reaches out to young carers from all communities throughout national and local programmes: **www.youngcarer.com**

STAND UP

This is about standing up for yourself, or on behalf of others who do not or cannot speak out for themselves. You might decide to:

- Join your support to a campaign that you believe in.

- Offer to stand beside a friend through a difficult time.

Invite the young people to commit to taking an action and to sharing their commitment with the group.

What action or actions have you committed to? How are you going to make a start?

The actions should be noted on the flipchart or record sheet. You will need to keep these notes safe to enable the group to look back next time to check what action has been carried out and to give continuity to the meetings.

REACH OUT AND LIVE LIFE!

Help the group to identify where they can make a difference.

Where can you make a difference as a group? Make a note to return to in Chapter Eight:

- Has this enquiry given you any ideas for your group project?

- Make a note in your book – ideas for group project.

- As individuals, commit to think and pray about your group project between now and the next session.

Invite the young people to give thought and prayer to the group project in the time between now and the next session.

PRAYER TIME

Light a candle in the middle of the room, with the young people sitting around in a circle. Remind the group that this is a sign of God's presence. Play some quiet music in the background.

BEAUTY WITHIN

Read by someone in the group.

ALEX'S STORY

Alex was taken to visit his grandma and grandad, who had a lovely garden with flowers that attracted beautiful butterflies from far and wide. Alex came across a chrysalis hanging on a shrub. His grandfather explained to him that the body of the caterpillar was transforming into an adult butterfly. Grandad explained that this was a miracle of nature and that after ten to fourteen days, what began as a caterpillar would struggle out of the chrysalis, and a beautiful butterfly would emerge. A transformation would take place;

"Just like in you and me," explained grandad.

"How so?", asked Alex.

"We grow and change every day. Sometimes it can be hard, but the beauty inside us is always there."

APPLICATION

Sometimes life can be tough, especially in times of change. However, within we are all children of God. No matter how we may sometimes feel, or how much of a struggle life might seem, God's plan for us is that we will become more than we, or others, can possibly imagine.

PRAYER

Pass around slips of paper and pens. Invite each of the young people to compose a prayer to place in a basket, which is then placed in the centre. Tell the group this is a time of quiet prayer and reflection, in which they may ask for God's direction in how to support someone in need, or how to ask someone for help if they are in need themselves.

Invite the group to say the following prayer together from their books:

CLOSING PRAYER

Father, pour out your Spirit

upon your young people,

and grant us

a new vision of your glory,

a new experience of your power,

a new faithfulness to your Word; and

a new consecration to your service,

that your love may grow in us,

and your kingdom come.

Through Christ our Lord.

Amen.

SOCIAL TIME

10-20 minutes.

RECORD SHEET

LEADING LIFE!

ADULT COMPANION'S REFLECTION

This chapter will help the group to explore the notion of Christian leadership – in the widest sense of the term. Young people are called to be fully responsible members of the Church in the world. They are called by God at their baptism, with a unique meaning and purpose which only they can fulfil. They are empowered to live this out by anointing and laying-on of hands at their confirmation.

During their teenage years, how young people live out their God-given purpose can be unclear. But they are called to put their Christian life into practice in the midst of their surroundings. To put it another way, they are called to be leaders in their own lives, and among their family, friends and peers.

The definition of "leadership" is used here in its widest sense. The young people are asked to look at examples of quiet, unassuming leadership alongside those of charismatic, assertive leaders, in order to encourage them to think of themselves in a leadership role.

Your role, like Eli directing Samuel to listen for the voice of the Lord (1 Samuel 3:1-10), is to encourage the young people to hear God calling them through the circumstances and events of their daily lives.

This has been a long journey for the adult companion and the group. In this penultimate chapter, an opportunity is offered for the young people to continue to meet over the following weeks, ideally through using Chapter Eight to support them in designing a group project to make a difference.

If you choose not to start the project, they may like to explore networks and youth activities in the Church. There are ideas in the Appendix for this. In particular they may wish to discuss affiliating with the YCW Impact movement which exemplifies the **SEE, JUDGE, ACT** approach which has been adopted in *Life*.

Invite the group to be quiet. Offer each person an opportunity to name an intention (such as a name or situation). Bring all these together in saying a prayer:

PRAYER

Father, pour out your Holy Spirit upon us your sons and daughters.

May we see with your eyes,

judge all things in your light

and act with love in our hearts.

Mould us into your apostles

full of joy and hope,

so that we can be the difference

and your kingdom come

and keep us under your protection.

Through Christ Jesus our friend and Saviour.

Amen.

There is an alternative prayer suggested in the last chapter of the young people's book:

PRAYER

Lord Jesus,

We thank you for this day.

We offer you all our hopes and struggles, joys and sorrows.

Help us to grow together in friendship,

so that our words and actions bear witness to you

and make a difference in people's lives.

We pray for our families, for those who are hungry, lonely, poor and homeless,

and for all who have asked for our prayers.

May you bless us with wisdom to care for the earth.

May you bless us in love to care for one another.

In your name may we make all things new.

Amen.

ICE-BREAKER – SALAD – LEADERS AND FOLLOWERS

Use the following ice-breaker, or another of your choice (a selection of alternatives can be found in the Appendices).

Arrange the chairs in a wide circle to allow for people to run between them. There should be enough chairs for everyone, minus one. Ask a volunteer to be the first "leader" and invite him or her to stand in the middle of the circle.

Ask the rest of the group – the "followers" – to each find a chair and sit on it. The leader calls out something which could apply to several people in the group, e.g., "Anyone who's wearing green trainers," or anyone who supports a particular football team, or watches a particular TV soap.

As soon as the call is made, anyone it applies to jumps up and rushes to another chair (but not the chair either side of them). The one person left standing then goes to the centre to start the process all over again.

If "Salad!" is called by the leader, everyone rushes to find another chair.

Remind everyone before you begin not to push or shove or dive for a chair.

NEWS ROUND

- What has happened to you this week?
- Share one fact from your week (a good or bad thing). What has made you think, caused you concern or given you reason to celebrate?

NOTE: If something significant comes up, it may be more important to follow it up than to complete today's enquiry. If you need to follow up on anything you can use the short enquiry approach found in the Appendices.

REVIEW

Invite the group to look at last week's record sheet or flipchart sheets. Ask the young people to share the results of their actions.

Look back at the last time you met. Hold one another to account:

- What individual or group actions did you decide upon?
- Were these actions carried out?
- If so, how did it go?

ENQUIRY

NOTE: If you complete an enquiry over several meetings, the Prayer, News Round and Review should be repeated at the beginning of each session.

ENQUIRY SUMMARY – SEE, JUDGE, ACT

Each enquiry has a central narrative, or flow, which can be summarised with a few questions. In each chapter we'll provide you with this summary to help you prepare and focus for your meetings:

SEE – What makes a leader in today's world?

JUDGE – How should we "lead" our lives as Christians?

ACT – How can we take responsibility for others?

SEE

As you begin the session, encourage everyone to take notes in their book. Ask someone to take notes on the record sheet or flipchart paper so that everyone can see it.

Invite the young person who is leading the session to begin with the **SEE**, where the group will look at their real experience.

- Where do you see leaders in society today? What makes them a leader?
- Could you be a leader? If so, what qualities do you have? If not, why not?

Many people think that leadership is all about having the skills and qualities to get people to follow. Surely a leader has to be persuasive, charismatic and able to speak in public. Of course there is that kind of leader, but sometimes leaders are quietly improving the world one step at a time, and inspiring others to do the same. Often it is these people who do the most.

Take, for example, the case of Katie Cutler, who hit the headlines in the north-east of England in 2015, after reading the story of Alan Barnes, a disabled pensioner whose collarbone had been broken when he was attacked outside his home. Shocked by what she read, Katie set up an online fundraising page and invited people to make donations. She inspired others to follow her example and without realising it she became a leader. Her gesture resonated with people everywhere and, as the donations poured in, they took on a significance which was greater than just money. Combined, so many individual acts of generosity came to symbolise kindness and compassion triumphing over one act of callousness and cruelty.

- Can you think of any further examples of people inspiring other people to make a difference?

- Do you know any others (friends, family or people in your community), who have led lives that support people, and inspire others?

QUIET INSPIRATION

You don't need to inspire thousands of people to donate money to a good cause to be a leader. John would never call himself a leader, but the choices he makes set him apart as an example for others to follow. John is at school, doing his GCSEs and coping with all the study, mock exams and revision. He also has the added responsibility of looking after his brother, David.

David has learning disabilities and lives at home with John and their mother. After their dad left home, their mother needed to go out to work, taking on extra shifts to help pay all the bills. John stays at home to look after David's needs. He ensures David has his dinner, and is supported to get to bed. Most of his evenings and weekends are taken up with helping his brother and cramming in school work. But John wouldn't have it any other way. He gets on with it, helping his mother and taking on responsibility for his brother.

John is quite private about his home life, but some people at school know how much John has to help out. His actions encourage his friends to be more understanding of people with learning disabilities, and of families

with complex situations. And John's example doesn't stop there. He has recently joined an online group for young carers, where he shares his own experience with other people in his situation. So John is inspiring his friends and strangers. They follow his example. He leads.

- Do you see leadership qualities in John?

- How does John show leadership?

- How do John's choices and actions inspire others?

- Do you know anyone like this?

JUDGE

This is the time when the young people explore what they think about these issues, what's good or bad about the situations, and what their faith says.

CARDINAL JOSEPH CARDIJN

Cardinal Joseph Cardijn lived in Belgium between 1882 and 1967. As a student he witnessed his father take on extra work into his old age, so that he could pay for Joseph to finish his studies. Harsh working conditions led to his father's death and, three years later, when Joseph was ordained a priest, he dedicated himself to supporting workers. Fr Cardijn knew well how powerless factory workers at the time felt – unable to have any say in their own lives. It became his mission to enable ordinary, working people – particularly the young – to realise that they could become influential and even aspire to leadership. In 1912 he began to work with factory workers, and eventually founded the Young Christian Workers, which today exists in Europe, Asia, Africa and South America, with a membership of over two hundred thousand young workers.

Have a look at the following quotes from Cardinal Cardijn on what it means to be a young leader:

- *"A young leader is a friend and companion to others, not someone giving orders; they are not a stranger but someone who shares the same difficulties."*

- *"What makes a leader? It is not an empty title nor is it merely an office. Being a leader is a quality and an aptitude. A leader is someone who has come to understand the responsibility they have in life towards their friends. They have an influence on those around them."*

- *"The call demands also that we should be witnesses to Christ. We must bear witness to Christ, not by words only, not just through our action, but also by the whole of our life... They must be a leader in their home, with their parents, brothers and sisters, at their place of work, when they go to lunch and when they speak to anyone."*

- What do you think of this view of leadership?

- Does it sound possible to be a witness to Christ in every aspect of your life by the way you act?

- Are you really prepared to take responsibility for yourself and for those around you? What would this mean?

NOTES

Invite a young person (who should have had a chance to prepare) to read the Gospel passage aloud. Ask the group to listen carefully to the story and think about the time, place and people involved.

Time allowing, it can be a good idea to invite a second young person to re-read the passage, although again ensure that she or he has had a chance to prepare it.

MATTHEW 20:25-28

But Jesus called them to him and said, "You know that the rulers of the Gentiles lord it over them, and their great ones are tyrants over them. It will not be so among you; but whoever wishes to be great among you must be your servant, and whoever wishes to be first among you must be your slave; just as the Son of Man came not to be served but to serve, and to give his life a ransom for many."

- Who is in this story and what happened?

- What was said? How do you think the people present would have reacted? Why?

Throughout the Gospels Jesus overturns the commonly held views of how we should think and behave. Much of what Jesus said would have surprised his listeners, especially as they began to hold him in higher and higher esteem; running around a lake to meet him on the other side, climbing a mount to listen to him, cheering him as he triumphantly entered Jerusalem. Here was a man they held up as a leader, even a king, but he encourages them to be the least amongst others and to be a servant. Perhaps the most shocking answer is his final answer. When Pilate challenges him to explain his kingship he picks up his cross and walks to Calvary to give his life for us. What model of leadership does this give us for today?

- What view of leadership does Jesus have?

- If we are to follow Jesus, how does this challenge us? What does "giving" our life look like today?

ACT

By committing to take action after we finish our enquiry we are saying that we want to make a difference in our lives and the lives of others. We are committing to living as disciples of Jesus.

The greatest among you will be your servant.

Matthew 23:11

In each chapter we will consider action in three categories:

HELP – *Helping others through service.*

TELL IT – *Making others aware of what we have discovered.*

STAND UP – *Standing up on behalf of others who do not or cannot speak out for themselves.*

As a group, think about a specific situation – probably from something you have been discussing today – which causes you concern. Could you – either as a group or as individuals – do anything to **HELP**, **TELL IT** or **STAND UP**?

HELP

This is about helping and supporting yourself and other people:

- Look at your Circle of Influence chart. Is there anyone on your chart in need of help? How can you be a young leader and show you take responsibility for others through your actions?

TELL IT

This is about raising awareness, or drawing people's attention to something they should be aware of:

- What issues have you discussed in your group? How can you show leadership by informing others about an issue important to you?

- Encourage people to get involved in supporting others. Who do you know who shows signs of leadership?

STAND UP

This is about standing up for yourself, or on behalf of others who do not or cannot speak out for themselves. You people might decide to:

- Look at your Circle of Influence chart. Is there anyone overlooked or silenced by others? Can you stand with them, to lend your voice to theirs? How?

- What local campaigns can you get involved in, you giving voice to an issue you are concerned about?

Invite the young people to commit to taking an action and to sharing their commitment with the group.

What action or actions have you committed to? How are you going to make a start?

The actions should be noted on the flipchart or record sheet. You will need to keep these notes safe to enable the group to look back next time to check what action has been carried out and to give continuity to the meetings.

REACH OUT AND LIVE LIFE!

Help the group to identify where they can make a difference.

Where can you make a difference as a group? Make a note to return to in Chapter Eight:

- Has this enquiry given you any ideas for your group project?

- Make a note in your book – ideas for group project.

- As individuals, commit to think and pray about your group project between now and the next session.

Invite the young people to give thought and prayer to the group project in the time between now and the next session.

If your group doesn't embark on a project together, you might want to consider registering with **IMPACT** (part of the Young Christian Workers), a Catholic organisation of teenagers who meet in groups across the world to **SEE**, **JUDGE**, **ACT**.

IMPACT can support you with more resources, visits to your group, and link you up with similar groups. See **www.ycwimpact.com**

PRAYER TIME

Light a candle in the middle of the room, with the young people sitting around in a circle. Remind the group that this is a sign of God's presence. Play some quiet music in the background.

MAKING AN IMPACT

Read by someone in the group.

> *Bringing the Gospel is bringing God's power to pluck up and break down evil and violence; to destroy and overthrow the barriers of selfishness, intolerance and hatred, so as to build a new world. Jesus Christ is counting on you! The Church is counting on you! The Pope is counting on you! May Mary, Mother of Jesus and our Mother, always accompany you with her tenderness: "Go and make disciples of all nations." Amen.*
>
> **Pope Frances' homily in Rio at World Youth Day, 2013**

APPLICATION

This call of Pope Francis is an invitation to young people to own their faith, to discipleship and a personal faith commitment. This is what *Life* has been about. The young people are journeying to move from a received to an owned faith. Faith is not ours to give – each young person must have their own personal conversion. We can only walk the walk with them on their faith journey. The rest is between them and God.

PRAYER

Pass around slips of paper and pens. Invite each of the young people to compose a prayer to place in a basket, which is then placed in the centre. Tell the group this is a time of quiet prayer and reflection, in which they may ask for God's direction in how to support someone in need, or how to ask someone for help if they are in need themselves.

Invite the group to say the following prayer together from their books:

CLOSING PRAYER

Father, pour out your Spirit

upon your young people,

and grant us

a new vision of your glory,

a new experience of your power,

a new faithfulness to your Word; and

a new consecration to your service,

that your love may grow in us,

and your kingdom come.

Through Christ our Lord.

Amen.

SOCIAL TIME

10-20 minutes.

RECORD SHEET

8

REACH OUT AND
LIVE LIFE!

ADULT COMPANION'S REFLECTION

This chapter is different to the previous chapters. Rather than offering a topic-based enquiry to be completed over a small number of meetings, this chapter will support the group to choose and devise a project together. This can be done over any number of meetings. It could be the main focus of the time together, or an additional activity to your meetings.

At this stage in the group's journey you should be continue with a familiar format to your meetings. A simple agenda could be:

PRAYER

NEWS ROUND

- What has happened to you this week?

- Share one fact from your week (a good or bad thing). What has made you think, caused you concern or given you reason to celebrate?

REVIEW

- What individual or group actions did you decide upon?

- Were these actions carried out?

- If so, how did it go?

ENQUIRY

- **SEE, JUDGE, ACT**

PRAYER TIME

SOCIAL TIME

Remember to prepare the meetings with the young person who will be leading the enquiry.

GETTING STARTED

This is a good exercise to begin with as it is crucial for the group listen to one another as they plan their project.

Ask the group to split up into pairs and sit facing each other. Space allowing, there should be a reasonable distance between each pair. One person then looks directly at their partner and talks for a minute or two about any topic which interests them (or a topic of your choice), while their partner pays no attention to what is being shared (avoiding eye contact, fiddling with hands, shuffling feet, looking decidedly bored, etc.)

The group then comes together and the speakers share how they felt at not being listened to. The group might then discuss what being a good listener means and why listening is important.

The effect can be exaggerated if the "speakers" are sent out of the room while the game is explained to the "listeners", so they don't know what to expect.

The group could then go back into pairs but this time the listening partner pays careful attention and asks sensible questions, to draw out the contrast.

ENQUIRY

SEE

In small groups discuss:

- What are the main issues, challenges or problems which became important to the group during the sessions?

- Are there any new issues facing you or the young people you know? Look at your Circle of Influence to help you think about this.

Choose the top three issues from your small group, to share with the larger group.

REPORT BACK

Explain to the rest of the group why you have chosen your three issues. Give examples.

You may want to note down the issues from the other small groups.

My friend Jules has been stopped three times after school by older boys from another school and had his phone stolen. The police don't seem too concerned if it's only a teenager this happens to.

Noah

What are you most concerned about? Your adult companion will help you identify the most pressing and important needs you have identified as a group.

Draw concentric circles on the floor or a large sheet of paper. Write down the issues on small pieces of paper or flags and place them around the outside edge of the circle. In turn, each small group moves an issue forward two spaces. You can also move back one space any issue that another group has moved. As you do so, explain your reasoning. Take time to discuss it and, if necessary, stop for prayer.

Stop when an issue reaches the centre.

JUDGE

- Why is it important to take action on our chosen issue, problem or challenge?

- What would Jesus say about this situation? Can you think of a relevant passage from the Gospels?

SCRIPTURE ENQUIRY

Let no one despise your youth, but set the believers an example in speech and conduct, in love, in faith, in purity.

1 Timothy 4:12

- What strikes you immediately about this passage?

- How are young people to set an example to others?

- What do you think this passage teaches us today?

THE ISSUE TREE

Now enquire in more depth into the issue you have settled on. Draw an **Issue Tree** on a flipchart. You can also note it below:

- What really happens in this issue? (Write on the trunk).

- Do you have any examples? Who was, or is, involved? How did, or do, the people involve feel? (Write on the branches).

- Why does this kind of thing happen? What are the causes? (The roots).

- What are the consequences? How are others affected by this situation? (The leaves).

ISSUE TREE

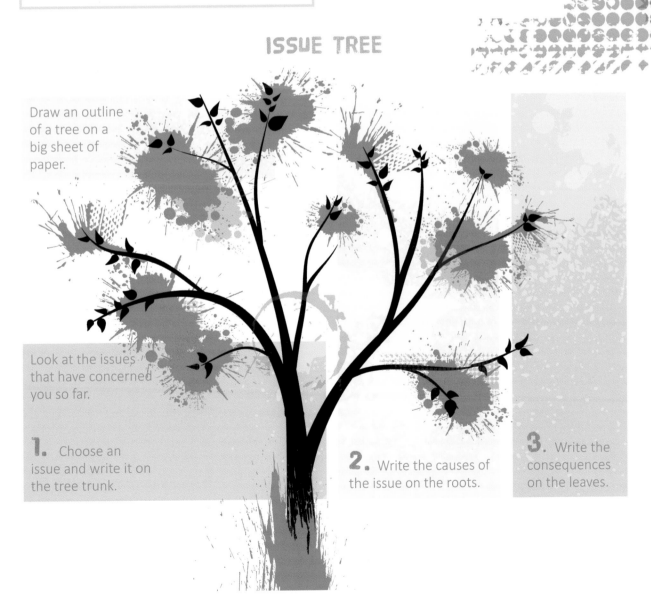

Draw an outline of a tree on a big sheet of paper.

Look at the issues that have concerned you so far.

1. Choose an issue and write it on the tree trunk.

2. Write the causes of the issue on the roots.

3. Write the consequences on the leaves.

GIFTS

- What gifts do you have in your group to do something about this situation?

- Add the gifts as fruits to your **Issue Tree**, so you can see all the resources you have available to help you in your project.

ACT

Serve one another with whatever gift each of you has received.

1 Peter 4:10

PERSONAL ACTION

Invite each person to contribute ideas as to what personal action they can take about the chosen issues.

- Can you as an individual **HELP**, **TELL IT** or **STAND UP** for others?

GROUP ACTION

What action can you take as a group? You don't have to do everything to solve the entire issue – but you can always do something together. Look back at the **Issue Tree**. Are there any causes or consequences that you can you do something about together?

What can we do together to **HELP** others, **TELL** others (raise awareness about the issue) or **STAND UP** for others?

PLAN OF ACTION

Create a **PLAN OF ACTION**. In your books (and on flipchart paper for all to see) write the following:

- The issue chosen by the group. Give it a project name.

- The aim of the project – what do you want to achieve? Why?

- Milestones – the steps that will get you there.

- The time plan. Alongside the name of the step, note the deadline and who will be responsible for that step.

- Contacts who can help – name these and their contact details. Look at your Circle of Influence to remind you who might help you.

- Make a financial plan under the headings "description", "income", and "expenditure".

Plan your group project using the blank pages in your book over the next few weeks. Review your progress each time the group meets.

PLAN OF ACTION

TITLE OF YOUR PROJECT

AIM OF PROJECT
WHAT DO YOU WANT TO ACHIEVE?
WHY?

MILESTONES
STEPS THAT WILL GET YOU THERE

TIME PLAN

DEADLINE	SUBJECT	PERSON IN CHARGE
_/_/_	_____	_____
_/_/_	_____	_____
_/_/_	_____	_____
_/_/_	_____	_____
_/_/_	_____	_____
_/_/_	_____	_____

CONTACTS WHO CAN HELP

NAME

FINANCIAL PLAN

DESCRIPTION   INCOME / EXPENSE

WHAT NEXT?

Consider registering with **IMPACT** (part of the Young Christian Workers), a Catholic organisation of teenagers who meet in groups across the world to **SEE**, **JUDGE**, **ACT**.

As a group, **IMPACT** can support you with more resources, visits to your group, and link you up with similar groups. See **www.ycwimpact.com**

There are also other suggestions for follow up in the Appendices.

To conclude this session, use the prayer of **IMPACT**, prayed by young people across the world.

PRAYER

Father, pour out your Holy Spirit upon us

your sons and daughters.

May we see with your eyes,

judge all things in your light

and act with love in our hearts.

Mould us into your apostles,

full of joy and hope,

so that we can be the difference

and your kingdom come

and keep us under your protection.

Through Christ Jesus our friend and Saviour.

Amen.

SOCIAL TIME

10-20 minutes.

RECORD SHEET

APPENDICES

ICE-BREAKERS

Use the following ice-breakers to help get your meeting started. Sometimes an ice-breaker can be used to introduce the theme of the session, but don't be overly concerned about always finding links – the ice-breakers can be simply fun ways of getting things going.

More ice-breakers can be found online. A quick search will reveal plenty. Or see the excellent: *New Youth Games Book*, by Alan Dearling and Howard Armsrong (Russell House, 1994, ISBN 1-898924-00-7)

SQUIRT

Invite everyone to stand in a circle with the "squirt master" in the centre. He or she then points at someone and yells "Squirt!" The person s/he aims at must duck, and at the same time the two on either side point at each other and shout "Squirt!" Of these three, whoever acts slowest is eliminated. The game goes to a shoot-out between the last two, who stand back to back and take several paces away from each other until the squirt master gives the signal to turn and fire.

RIVER CROSSING

The group divides into teams or splits into two. The teams line up next to each other against one wall. Each team is then given sheets of newspaper. The object is for the whole team to get from one side of the room to the other without touching the floor with the aid of the newspaper. If anyone is spotted touching the floor they have to go back and begin again. The firsts team across is the winner. How many sheets of paper are given to each team depends upon the area to be traversed. Usually three or four sheets will be enough.

TRUST WALK

This game is for groups where the young people know and have confidence in one another. A member of the group is blindfolded and stands at one end of the room. Chairs or other suitable objects are place around the room but not too close together. The person who is blindfolded then has to get from one end of the room to the other by following instructions from group members who will be positioned around the room. The exercise can then be debriefed either in terms of the trust involved.

MUMMIES

And for something completely different...

Divide the young people into groups of about four. Each group receives a toilet roll and is asked to create a mummy within a set amount of time (around four minutes) by wrapping one of the group in the toilet paper. The adult companion should judge the dummies for the best/scariest mummy. A prize may be given. The group should then think about and share how well they worked together as a group.

SHORT ENQUIRIES

The following guides for preparing your own enquiries are general questions that can be linked to an enquiry into a particular issue. They can also be used as follow-ups to anything specific and/or challenging which may have arisen during the News Round part of the meeting.

First, some general questions you could use to get the discussion going:

SEE

- Describe the experience.

- Who was involved?

- What actually happened?

- Where does/did this take place?

- When does/did it happen?

- How often does/did this occur?

- How do you feel about it?

- What kind of things were said on this occasion?

- Why does this happen? What are the causes?

- What are the consequences?

JUDGE

- What do you think about this?

- Do you think this is right or wrong? Is it good or bad? Why/why not?

- Should things be any different? How?

- Is this the way we should treat people? If not, why not?

- How does being a Christian make a difference in this situation?

- Did Jesus teach or show us anything about this?

- How do you think Jesus would have done or said in response this situation?

As the adult companion, you may want to introduce a relevant scripture text here. You can use general questions, for example:

- Who is in this story and what happened?

- What was said? How do you think the people present would have reacted? Why?

- Does this story have anything to say to us about the situation we are considering today?

Here are a few texts that may be of help:

- **Parables**: Luke 10:25-37 ; Luke 14:15-24; Luke 15:1-7; Luke 15:8-10; Luke 15:11-31; Luke 16:19-30; Luke 18:9-14

- **Teaching and values**: Matthew 5:1-12; Matthew 5:38-48; Matthew 6:19-21. 24; Matthew 7:12-14; Mark 10:23-27

- **Prayer**: Matthew 6:5-6; Matthew 6:7-15; Matthew 7:7-11; Luke 18:1-8

- **Call and mission of the disciples**: Matthew 4:18-21; Matthew 9:9-13; Mark 6:7-13; Luke 5:1-11

- **Following Christ**: Matthew 5:13-16; Matthew 9:35-37; Mark 9:33-37; Mark 10:41-45; Luke 1:26-38; Luke 6:46-49

- **Feeding the hungry**: Mark 6:30-44

ACT

The **ACT** will flow from the **SEE** and **JUDGE**. Action can be simple and straightforward - such as befriending someone, changing personal habits and behaviour, finding out more about something or a situation – or more complex, something that involves careful thought and planning. It can be personal or group action. It should be relevant to what has been shared, achievable and Christian in character. There are three main types of action:

- **HELP** – Helping others through service.

- **TELL IT** – Making others aware of what you have discovered.

- **STAND UP** – Standing up on behalf of others who do not or cannot speak out for themselves.

Plans for action should be noted and followed up at the next meeting in order to ensure that the group does not become a talking shop.

REVIEWING

All the **SEE**, **JUDGE** and **ACT** in the world is worth nothing if we don't reflect on and learn from it. Therefore, reviewing is always important. To review actions together, here are some questions you can use with the group:

- What action did you take?

- How did you feel about it before and afterwards?

- Was it difficult or easy to do what you'd decided? Why?

- Who else was involved?

- What effect did you're action have on others?

- Were there any surprising effects?

- What did you learn about yourself?

- Is there any further action to be taken?

TOPIC-BASED ENQUIRIES

BE YOURSELF

This enquiry may support you in following up issues that arise in Chapter Three.

SEE

- In what situations do the young people you know find themselves most relaxed and at ease? Can you give some actual examples?

- What is your own experience? When do you feel most relaxed?

- When do you find that your friends pretend to be something they are not? Can you give examples from your own experience?

- How is your dress, taste in music, political opinion, religious view affected by others?

- Are your friends affected by your opinion of others? Why?

JUDGE

- Is it good or bad to be one of the crowd? Give reasons.

- Is it a good thing or not to put on an act? Give reasons.

- To whom should you be prepared to listen, to form your opinions?

Let us look at the teaching of Jesus - Luke 14:7-11:

- What does this passage tell us about people pretending to be what they're not?

ACT

- Do any of the situations you have discussed require action? If so, who should act and how?

- Can everyone think of a definite action they can take? e.g., being prepared to defend a personal point of view; being willing to listen to someone you respect; being more honest in a particular situation.

PORNOGRAPHY

This enquiry may support you in following up issues that arise in Chapter Three and Chapter Five. There are several good websites which can help, such as: **www.theporneffect.com**

SEE

- Do you know of young people of your age who access pornography? How and where do they do this, e.g., online, on TV, in magazines?

- Do they or you talk about it? Do they think it's okay?

- Are their parents aware of what they are doing?

- What effect do you think pornography has on the way young people may view sex and relationships?

JUDGE

Statistics show that most teenagers have used the internet to access porn.

- What do you think about this?

- Many would say that pornography can be addictive. Do you think this is true? What are the consequences of being addicted to something?

- Why do people make and sell pornography? Do you think it is okay? Why/why not?

- Porn is a multi-billion pound industry. How do you think those making money out of it view the women and men exhibited in the porn?

Do you not know that your body is a temple of the Holy Spirit... ?

1 Corinthians 6:19

- What do you think about this teaching from St Paul?

- Do you think using pornography is okay for a Christian?

- What do you think is God's plan for sexual relationships?

- Where have you heard about abortion?

- Do you know of anyone who has had an abortion?

- Do your friends ever talk about it? What do they say?

- What does the law state about abortion?

- What are the reasons a woman might give for having an abortion?

- What do you think some of the consequences of having an abortion may be?

JUDGE

Every civil law is based on the recognition of the first and most fundamental right, the right to life.

Pope Francis, 11 April 2014

- What do you think of the quote from Pope Francis?

- What reasons do people give for opposing abortion?

- The Catholic Church teaches that human life begins at conception, the very moment of fertilisation, and that it is our duty to respect and preserve life from conception to a natural death. What do you think of this?

- Why might some women, and sometimes their partners, feel that they have no option but to have an abortion?

- What options besides abortion are there for women facing an unexpected or unwanted pregnancy?

ACT

- Is it possible to avoid viewing and/or becoming addicted to pornography? How?

- Is there anyone to talk through any difficulties we may have in this area?

- Can prayer be helpful? What kind of prayer would help?

- When things go wrong, where can a Christian go to get forgiveness, healing and spiritual help?

Many young people and adults are in danger of becoming isolated in their consumption of lewd pictures, films, and internet services instead of finding love in a personal relationship. Loneliness can lead to a blind ally in which masturbation becomes an addiction.

YouCat, 409

RESPECT FOR LIFE

This enquiry may support you in following up issues that arise in Chapter Five.

It would be a good idea to do some research about abortion and the law in advance. More information and resources that may help you with this enquiry can be found on the websites of **LIFE**: **http://lifecharity.org.uk**, and SPUC (Society for the Protection of Unborn Children): **www.spuc.org.uk**

ACT

- Is there anyone we know who could benefit from someone to talk to about this issue or who is in need of help?

- What can we do to ensure that our own local community, school or parish would be welcoming and supportive of women who become pregnant and young mothers?

It is poverty to decide that a child may die so that you can live as you wish.

Mother Teresa

CATHOLIC SOCIAL TEACHING – THE CHURCH'S BEST-KEPT SECRET

This enquiry may support you in following up issues that arise in Chapters Seven and Eight.

Million Minutes provides materials to groups to explore the six principles of Catholic Social Teaching: **www.millionminutes.org**. CAFOD's youth website: **www.cafod.org/education**

SEE

- What problems and issues are facing you, your family members or friends at the moment? For example, unemployment, poor working conditions (e.g., low pay, working a zero-hours contract, being required to work long hours without suitable breaks), high rents and poor living conditions?

- Can you give facts and examples? (These should be carefully noted.)

- Do you keep up with the news? How widespread are the issues we have looked at?

JUDGE

- Have you heard of Catholic Social Teaching? If not can you Google it on a smartphone?

    The Gospel is about the Kingdom of God... it is about loving God who reigns in our world. To the extent that he reigns within us, the life of society will be a setting for universal fraternity, justice, peace and dignity. Both Christian preaching and life, then, are meant to have an impact on society.

    Pope Francis, "The Joy of the Gospel", 180

- What do we think of these words from Pope Francis? What does he mean?

The Church gives us a set of principles, or guidelines, to help us live our Christian life and to have "an impact on society"? Read through the summary of the principles of Catholic Social Teaching:

PRINCIPLES OF CATHOLIC SOCIAL TEACHING

Dignity and equality of each human person: *Everyone is equal. They're lovingly made in God's image and likeness. The other principles flow from this.*

Participation and community: *Human beings exist in relation to one another. We're called to live with others, to participate, to join in, to work alongside others for the good of all.*

A preferential option for the poor: *Jesus gives us the example of putting the poor first, giving them special importance, thinking of their needs and enabling them to have their rightful place in the world. It is more than just helping the poor. We must enable those living in poverty to play a full, active role in society and help their voice be heard.*

The dignity and rights of workers: *Human beings are not something to be owned and used, or a tool as part of a process to make things. Human beings are greater than any thing. They have the right to have a job, to be valued, to contribute to the building up of good in the world, to earn money and so support their family.*

Solidarity among people and the promotion of peace: *We seek the good of one another, aware of our dependence on one another. Pope John Paul II said, "Solidarity is a firm and persevering determination to commit oneself to the common good." Peace flows from this. We are called to live honestly with one another, working together in love for the good of all. This is what will lead to true peace.*

Care for the earth: *Often the way we treat creation leads to the harm of it, and of those living on it. Our destruction of the earth for quick gain has repercussions on the natural world, ourselves, and generations to come. We need to treat the earth with respect.*

- What do you think about them?

- How might they help you consider some of the issues you discussed in your **SEE**?

- How could they help you to make decisions in your daily life? How might they help you to make choices about the big decisions on life, such as university, career, who to vote for when you turn eighteen?

ACT

- Can we take action on any of the problems which were raised in the **SEE** part of our meeting today?

- Is there a Justice and Peace group in the parish? Does everyone know what a Justice and Peace group is, what they do or what action they take? Give examples. Can you invite someone from the parish Justice and Peace group (or another parish nearby) to speak about what they do and about Catholic Social Teaching?

- Can you share with anyone in your Circle of Influence what you have discovered today? Feed back on this next week.

RESPONSIBILITY – TAKING A LEAD AND MAKING A CHANGE

This enquiry may support you in following up issues that arise in Chapter Seven.

SEE

- What sort of responsibility do you and your friends have at home? At school, at college? Give examples. How do you feel about these responsibilities?

- What do you feel about being in charge of something?

- Do you know any situation where a young person has felt helpless to change a situation?

- Can you think of any occasions recently when your behaviour or conversation had changed a situation?

- How do changes for good usually come about?

JUDGE

- Do you carry out your responsibilities well?

- Are there things you would like to be responsible for but are not allowed to be?

- Are there some things you would like to avoid being responsible for?

- Do you think your behaviour, conversation, opinions and prayers could make a difference to situations at home, in your leisure time, parish, etc.?

- What would you like to see changed?

Let us look at the teaching of Jesus – Matthew 25:19-21:

- What does this tell us about the importance of small responsibilities?

ACT

- Is there one responsibility you have, which you could take more seriously?

- Is there a situation which you could help to change for the better? Commit to taking responsibility for something which will make a difference for others.

- A small action is infinitely better than none. Use your conversation and behaviour to influence somebody this week.

RESOURCES

The best source of support is from others also working with young people in your local area. Contact your diocesan youth office to see what activities (such as training and resource days) are organised for volunteers, youth ministers and youth workers in your diocese or deanery.

WEBSITES

See the Catholic Youth Ministry Federation (CYMFed) website to find the local contact details for your diocese: **www.cymfed.org.uk**

The Young Christian Workers and Impact provide help to set up and support groups using the **SEE**, **JUDGE**, **ACT** model: **www.ywcimpact.com**

For an excellent website that brings together information, resources and advice, see: **www.catholicyouthwork.com**

CaFE provides audiovisual resources to support you in your work with young people, such as "Plugged In", "Deeper – Why Jesus?" and "Amazing Gift". See: **www.faithcafe.org**

Southwark Catholic Youth Services has produced "Life in Christ", featuring 45 short videos with insights and catechetical introductions from a wide range of contemporary Catholic theologians and scripture scholars. See: **www.scys.org.uk**

Million Minutes provides resources and activities for young people based on the principles of Catholic Social Teaching. See: **www.millionminutes.org**

They also host the Celebrating Young People Awards, which celebrate the contribution of young people from within our Catholic communities to making a difference in the world. Why not nominate some of your young people who have taken action during *Life*: **www.millionminutes.org/awards**

BOOKS

FOR THE ADULT COMPANION

Catholic Bishop's Conference of England and Wales Department of Evangelisation and Catechesis, *Called to a Noble Adventure* (Catholic Youth Ministry Federation/CYMFED). ISBN 978-0-9571906-03

FOR THE YOUNG PEOPLE

John Chater, *The Survival Guide for Young Catholics* (2015, Redemptorist Publications). ISBN 9780852314241

Fr Stephen Wang, *A Way of Life for Young Catholics* (CTS). ISBN 978-1-86082-487-6

YOUCAT – Youth Catechism of the Catholic Church (CTS Ignatius Press). ISBN 978-1-86082-728-0

YOUCAT Youth Prayer Book (CTS Ignatius Press). ISBN 978-1-86082-852-2

There are many Catholic youth bibles available. Go online or browse your local Catholic bookshop for the right bible for your group.

There are also many praise and worship CDs out there to support young people's participation in prayer time, especially when musicians are not available. "The Best New Worship Songs Ever" is a three-CD box set which you will find useful for the prayer sessions in *Life*. Go online or browse your local Christian bookshop.

EVENTS

The group will benefit from taking part in Church events such as World Youth Day (age permitting) and local deanery or diocesan youth events. (Find contact details for your diocese at **www.cymfed.org.uk**).

There are also national festivals for young people, such as Brightlights: **www.brightlights.org.uk** and youth events organised by communities such as the Sion Community: **www.sionyouth.org.uk**

Youth streams are included in larger events such as New Dawn in the Church: **www.newdawn.org.uk**, and Celebrate: **www.celebrateconference.org**